How to Solve
Your PEOPLE
PROBLEMS

How to Solve *Your* PEOPLE PROBLEMS

Dr. Alan Godwin

HARVEST HOUSE PUBLISHERS

EUGENE, OREGON

All Scripture quotations are taken from The Message. Copyright © by Eugene H. Peterson 1993, 1994, 1995, 1996, 2000, 2001, 2002. Used by permission of NavPress Publishing Group.

Published in association with Rosenbaum & Associates Literary Agency, Inc., Brentwood, Tennessee.

Harvest House Publishers and the author(s) have made every effort to trace the ownership of all poems and quotes. In the event of a question arising from the use of a poem or quote, we regret any error made and will be pleased to make the necessary correction in future editions of this book.

Cover photo © Digital Vision / Getty Images

Cover by Dugan Design Group, Bloomington, Minnesota

HOW TO SOLVE YOUR PEOPLE PROBLEMS
Copyright © 2008 by Alan Godwin
Published by Harvest House Publishers
Eugene, Oregon 97402
www.harvesthousepublishers.com

Library of Congress Cataloging-in-Publication Data

Godwin, Alan
How to solve your people problems / Alan Godwin.
   p. cm.
ISBN-13: 978-0-7369-2351-4

1. Conflict management—Religious aspects—Christianity. 2. Interpersonal relations—Religious aspects—Christianity. I. Title.
BV4597.53.C58G63 2008
158.2—dc22

2008001042

Printed in the United States of America

10 11 12 13 14 15 16 / VP-NI / 10 9 8 7 6 5 4 3 2

To my wife...
An old professor of mine once said that we learn the most
not in the classroom but in the laboratory of life.
Penny has been my "lab partner" for more than 30 years.
I've been privileged to watch her live wisely
and to have her teach me most of what I know about
what makes relationships work the way God intended.
To her I am eternally grateful.

Acknowledgments

This book could not have been written and published without the significant contributions of numerous individuals. I have many to thank.

I appreciate my clients—people who've inspired me by their courage and willingness to grow. The ideas in this book aren't just theories. They work. I'm certain of that because I've seen people apply these principles to their real-life conflict situations with great results. Sometimes clients thank me for helping them. I usually respond, "I'm just the guy on the sidelines wearing the headset. You're the player on the field taking the hits. Thanks for letting me learn by watching you play." I really mean that.

I'm indebted to friends and family members who took time out of their busy schedules to read my manuscript when it was full of mistakes, incoherencies, and typos. They laboriously read it, marked it up, gave useful feedback, and provided encouragement. They helped me chisel off some rough edges, and for that I thank them. A special thank you to my wife, Penny, who graciously helped me think through the reflection questions that accompany each chapter.

I owe a debt of gratitude to Bucky Rosenbaum, my literary agent who has patiently guided this neophyte through the unfamiliar territory of book publishing. Early on, he encouraged me by expressing his belief in this project. I've appreciated his wisdom, his depth of experience, his gentle tolerance of newcomer questions, and his friendship. Thanks, Bucky.

I'd like to thank the wonderful people at Harvest House Publishers. All of the good things I heard about them prior to meeting them proved to be true. My special thanks to Terry Glaspey, who originally caught the vision for what I wanted to communicate in this book. And to my editor, Barb Gordon, who painstakingly molded the manuscript into its better and smoother version. I'd also like to thank the entire Harvest House team for their help and support.

I want to especially thank my family. I'm a morning person living with a bunch of night people. That's a good thing because I was able to work early while they slept late. Even still, they've been incredibly patient and consistently encouraging.

Finally, thanks to all the coffee shops of the world that allow people to plug in their laptops and take up space for long stretches of time.

CONTENTS

GOOD CONFLICT CAMP

As a clinical psychologist in private practice, I spend much of my time watching conflict or hearing about it. Over the years, it's been my observation that adults often argue like children. Having begun my practice when my kids were in elementary school, I was sitting in my office one day listening to a client describe a workplace dispute and thought, *This sounds exactly like what I hear at the end of the day when my kids tell me about playground squabbles. The only difference is the age of the combatants.* Another client told me, "When I retire, I'm planning to open a daycare center just to remind me of work." Another client introduced himself and said, "I work at (name of firm), also known as 'Adult Kindercare.'" I frequently hear arguments between adults in my office that sound like: "Did too...did not...did too...did not."

Everyone starts off fighting like children, but some people never grow up in this area. They are brilliant when it comes to making a living but brainless when it comes to solving personal conflict problems. They've earned advanced degrees from the University of Conflict Avoidance but flunked Conflict Resolution Kindergarten. They teach fair fighting rules at work but fight like cats and dogs at home. And if they go to church on Sunday, they act out their disunifying immaturities in a setting supposedly known for its unity. In short, people have people problems but don't know what to do about them. Or if they do know what to do, they often can't figure out how to implement what they know. Consequently, I've often wished I could send my clients to Good Conflict Camp. If such a place existed, they could learn the ABCs of conflict resolution, practice arguing like adults, and return to my office better able to resolve the conflicts that brought them there in the first place. In a sense, this book is the curriculum I would use for Good Conflict Camp.

Much of the content of this book has been derived from two sources: observations of people doing conflict the bad way and observations of people doing it the good way. I've seen lots of the bad kind, having watched it, heard about it, and practiced it myself. But there actually are people who do conflict a good way. They seem to have mastered the art of solving people problems well. How do they do that?

We'll address this in the chapters to come by looking at how and why conflict goes badly and what needs to happen for it to go well. By the book's end, it is my hope you'll understand four essential truths.

Truth 1: Close relationships involve conflict.

We all want and need people connections. But when we get connected to people, we inevitably have problems with people. Our imperfections rub against each other and friction occurs. The closer the contact, the greater the conflict potential. No matter what the setting—in marriage, at work, at school, in friendships, in families, at church—people connections involve people problems. We may not like it, but it happens.

Truth 2: Relationships work well only when conflict is handled well.

Relational success has less to do with what we have in common and more to do with how well we work through our differences. The absence of conflict is impossible, but successfully working through differences is achievable. This is called *good conflict*. Good conflict enables us to grow personally and to enjoy the benefits that relationships are designed to provide.

Truth 3: We naturally handle conflict poorly.

The trouble is, most of us don't argue well and are naturally inclined toward *bad conflict,* which allows for few if any differences to be resolved when its methods are used. It's what happens when we do what comes naturally. The results are personal stagnation and relational alienation.

Truth 4: Conflict with reasonable and unreasonable people must be handled differently.

Bad conflict comes naturally, but good conflict can be learned. In this book you'll discover how to achieve good conflict with two types of people: *reasonable* and *unreasonable.* Reasonable people have what unreasonable people lack—effective reasoning abilities. Good conflict methods used with reasonable people won't work with unreasonable people, so alternative methods must be employed.

I had an injury once that required surgical repair. I was somewhat skeptical about the necessity of it until the orthopedist showed me the X-rays. "See that right there?" he asked. "That's what we have to go in and fix." An actual physical view of the problem caused my skepticism to vanish. Later, I thought, *I wish I could produce X-rays of people's emotions or conflict patterns so they could tangibly observe what needs repairing. That would make the process easier to grasp and more concrete.* Concepts such as bad conflict, good conflict, reasonableness, and unreasonableness are very real, but nonphysical things are sometimes hard to comprehend. I've employed various methods throughout the book to make the concepts more tangible. I'll illustrate the ideas using examples from literature, history, music, television, and movies.

To avoid a maze of case studies, I'll primarily tell two stories—one about conflict between two reasonable people and the other about a client's conflict with an unreasonable person. As we explore a principle, we'll also discover how these people learned and made use of it to change their conflict systems from bad to good. While all the details are factually accurate, the stories are composites of similar cases. So don't be surprised if some of what you read sounds like you.

In addition, reflection questions accompany each chapter to help you consider ways to apply the content, making it less academic and more relevant to your world where conflict happens.

Throughout life, we frequently come in contact with what might be called *conflict truisms*—things an older or wiser person might tell us about fighting or getting along with people:

- Don't go to bed angry.
- You can't reason with unreasonable people.
- You catch more flies with molasses than with vinegar.
- Don't poke a hornet's nest.
- Don't wear your feelings on your sleeve.
- Consider the source.
- Keep your friends close and your enemies closer.

These maxims have stood the test of time and impart relational wisdom that we all would do well to heed. I'll make frequent reference to these truisms and place them into a larger framework so we can better understand their significance and be more apt to apply them.

There was a certain tension I experienced in writing this book. On one hand I wanted to share something more detailed and descriptive than grocery store magazine articles on fighting fair. On the other hand, who wants to read a book about something as negative as conflict? Hopefully, I've made the subject matter comprehensive enough to be useable, concise enough to be readable, and positive enough to be interesting.

It would be presumptuous to suggest that the ideas and methods presented here are new. The concepts have been around for a long time. In "The Repair Shop" section, we'll look at what a 3,000-year-old document—the book of Proverbs—has to say about bad conflict, good conflict, and how to handle reasonable and unreasonable people.

My purpose has been to make these principles easy to understand and implement.

Finally, many of my examples are of marital problems because much of my time is spent in counseling couples. But the principles apply just as well to conflicts at work, at school, between parents and children, at church, in the neighborhood, between friends, in the extended family, or in any setting where people interact.

Section 1

PEOPLE AND PROBLEMS

Two renowned "anthropologists" made statements that sum up the ideas presented in this section. The first anthropologist, Pearl Bailey, once noted, "What the world really needs is more love and less paperwork." She was right about that. The fact is that all of us need love and spend a lot of time and energy pursuing connections. We're wired for relationships and fail to thrive when isolated from others.

But when we get close to others we have problems. The second anthropologist, Charles Schultz, made this statement through Linus in his *Peanuts* comic strip: "I love humanity. It's people I can't stand." When we achieve those pursued connections, we inevitably discover that people problems are part of the package. If the problems are handled well *(good conflict)*, then the relationships turn out to be worth the pursuit. If handled poorly *(bad conflict)*, the relationships fail to provide us with what we need and want. Hence, relationships work well only when conflict is handled well.

There are two types of conflict, but there are also two types of people: *reasonable* and *unreasonable*. Reasonable people have "reasoning abilities," while unreasonable people don't. Consequently, these two groups of people must be handled differently. Section 2 (Chapters 3 through 5) gives a detailed description of how to achieve good conflict with reasonable people, while Section 3 (Chapters 6 through 8) discusses good conflict with people who are unreasonable.

The concepts introduced in this section—two types of conflict and two types of people—lay the foundation for everything else discussed in this book. Having good relationships necessitates handling people problems the good way—with both groups of people.

Chapter 1

DEALING WITH PORCUPINES

Why love if loving hurts so much?
We love to know that we are not alone.
C.S. LEWIS

Just as lotions and fragrance give sensual delight,
a sweet friendship refreshes the soul.
PROVERBS 27:9

It was a big day for me. I had recently passed the driving test—on the second attempt, I might add—and successfully convinced my mother to let me take her blue Pontiac to school. In my mind's eye I pictured this occasion unfolding this way. First, I would pull up to the school and park. Then, as I emerged from the vehicle, groups of girls would gather and watch from a distance, impressed beyond words, yearning deeply for the chance to date me. Members of the "in group" would say to each other, "We need to ask that guy to hang out with us. Man, he is so cool." Driving the car to school would be my ticket to popularity.

Assured that all had gone as planned, I smugly took my seat in first period, having confidently crossed the threshold into the world of Cooldom. Just then we heard the principal over the intercom. He said, "May I have your attention please. May I have your attention please. There is a blue Pontiac parked on Riverside Drive. The doors are locked, and the motor is running." The class I was in exploded in raucous laughter, as did other classes up and down the hallway. "What kind of idiot would do that?" some questioned. "What a goob!" others exclaimed.

For a fleeting few seconds I considered joining in to ridicule this anonymous nitwit. *No way I'm going to admit to this,* I internally reasoned. *I'll leave it running. It'll probably just run out of gas.* But then the little sense I did possess kicked in, and I walked to the front of the classroom to confess the car was mine. My teacher displayed a mixture of graciousness mixed with an "I'm so glad I'm not you" attitude. As I ran the gauntlet to the principal's office, people were still racked with laughter, and I heard words such as "nincompoop" and "loser." I was told later that my friends (I use that term loosely) in other classes all loudly proclaimed, "Godwin! That's Alan Godwin's car." For a single day I had the dubious distinction of being the most conspicuous person at school—but not in the manner I'd hoped. My mom wasn't so pleased either.

At times, what we desire the most—personal relationship—is the source of our greatest consternation. I was thrilled about taking the car to school that day, not because I liked driving it—it was a powder-blue Pontiac Catalina, for crying out loud. Instead, I was pumped about the relationship enhancement possibilities. My motivation had not been automotive but relational. And the discomfort I felt for the rest of that day had little to do with understanding the potential car damage and everything to do with the damage done to my esteem in the eyes of others. Relationships fulfill us the most, but they can also hurt us the most.

John Ortberg talks about the "dance of the porcupines":[1] A desire for connection draws us toward people, but the fear of hurt causes both of us to stick out "quills" for protection. The pain of getting poked causes us to move away. Alternating between moving in and moving out is the dance. Let's look now at the individual dance steps and what must happen to alter the pattern.

Moving In

Understanding the fundamental need for connection, many songwriters have penned lyrics that reflect this deep human longing. That's why our radios are flooded with romance songs that say I can't live without you, I can't get enough of you, I'm only happy when we're together, and I'm not a whole person without you.

Throughout our lifespans, we need and desire what psychologists refer to as *attachment,* a bonding with another person. Infants need attachment so much that depriving them of it may result in death. Adoptive parents are warned about possible difficulties if an adopted child's early attachments were deficient. As we proceed through the developmental stages, we relish inclusion but hate being excluded. We form friendships, join clubs or teams, enroll in associations, join fraternities or sororities, go to parties, hang out together, visit chat rooms, text message each other, connect ourselves to the worldwide web, date, get married, and attend family gatherings. Some people join gangs. Others join churches, sing in choirs, enroll in small groups, serve on committees, and travel with others on short-term mission projects. We yell with others at sporting events, laugh together at comedy clubs, and cry together at funerals. We're intrigued by TV shows that portray friendships and bars where "everybody knows your name." Ex-soldiers recall fondly the deep friendships formed in times of battle. Retiring athletes talk about how much they'll miss the locker room camaraderie.

If we get sick, studies show that restoration of health is facilitated by healthy interpersonal connections. At the time of death, we prefer to be surrounded by those we love. From one end of life to the other, we spurn loneliness and seek the company of others. The "moving in" step of the dance is driven by this universal need to attach.

Getting Poked

But when we attach ourselves to someone, we invariably discover that this sought-after object of attachment has flaws and rough edges that hurt when encountered. Indeed, there is something "wrong" with all of us. Psychologists call it "abnormal psychology" or "psychopathology," while theologians call it the "fallenness of man" or "depravity." Most of us use colloquial terms like "screwed up" to express it. Someone once said, "There's a little larceny in us all." We are imperfect people living in an imperfect world with other imperfect people. We're drawn to people's positives but experience their negatives when we move in close. And coming in contact with those negatives can hurt.

While romance music expresses our attachment wishes, some country music songs speak to the pain experienced when affections turn sour. I once heard a few spoofs on country songs that expressed these notions: "Now that we're so miserable, I hope you're happy," "She chews tobacco but she won't choose me," and "Ain't been no trash in my trailer since the night I kicked you out."

Anticipating the potential pain of connection, we instinctively stick out quills for protection, the internal thought being, *If I let you in too close, I could get hurt.*

When we move in, we eventually get poked, and then we move out.

Moving Out

We crave attachments but hate pain, so we move out. For protection purposes, we distance ourselves from relationship—the very thing we desire the most. This strategic maneuver of using "relational geography" is displayed in several common renditions.

Buffered Connections

The basic stance here is, *It's OK for us to be close, but not that close. We're not going to talk about it, but I only let people in just so far.* These people have relational moats and drawbridges they use to deny access to their castle's inner sanctum.

I once watched a TV interview with a noted public figure and his wife. When the questions turned personal, his wife said, "Most people see my husband as friendly, gregarious, and warm. And that's true. But what people don't see is the steel wall that drops when you get in close. We've been married for a long time, and even I have never seen on the other side of that wall." The intrigued interviewer turned to the man and asked him to comment, at which point the camera framed the interview subject's head and shoulders. He paused, stammered, and began talking about his public achievements. The interviewer interrupted him and repeated her request for him to elaborate on his wife's comments. The camera then zoomed in for a face shot only. Once again he paused and then began waxing eloquent about his career accomplishments. The television audience got a chance to see for themselves the very wall his wife described.

Walls aren't bad as long as they have gates. In healthy relating, we need walls and gates to let some in, to let some in closer, to let a small number in very close, and to keep others out. But for some people "we'll do fine as long as we keep our distance" is the unspoken relational imperative that governs most or all of their relationships.

Pretend Closeness

Here the thought is, *Real relationships are way too risky. Let's have make-believe intimacy for a while. What do you say? That way, nobody gets hurt.* This is the philosophical underpinning of "friends with benefits," the casual hook-up, or the one-night stand.

Anesthetized Connections

Since actual, up-close relationships involve pain at times, some people numb the pain with pain-numbing substances that serve as relational lubricants. *Closeness requires anesthesia to kill the pain if something goes wrong,* the thinking goes. Little wonder, then, that drinking holes often double as popular pick-up spots.

Purposeful Distance

When families move frequently, some kids sidestep attachments to avoid the pain of detaching. They deliberately keep their distance because they know how much it hurts to lose friendships. Soldiers sometimes purposely decide not to get close to other soldiers, having experienced the pain of losing comrades in battle. Some people deliberately isolate themselves from others to avoid the complexities of relationships.

There was a time when most houses were built with front porches, a place where neighbors could sit and visit. Now we're more likely to build houses with privacy decks that hinder us from knowing our neighbors.

Vicarious Closeness

I get my closeness needs met by watching others do it. That way I don't get hurt. Some people are spectators in the stands watching characters from pop culture, television, movies, and books taking hits on the relational field of play. Another form of this is pornography, in which paying customers substitute contrived connections for ones that are real.

Techno Connections

I've been burned so often in person that I prefer cyber-anonymity. It seems safer and quicker and, if I encounter a loser, I can always hit delete. In some ways technology is a means of connecting with others. But some people use it for protection, a way to form what they perceive to be low-risk attachments.

Moving Back In

Distancing, in whatever form it takes, protects us from pain. But it gets lonely out there. Eventually we move back in, seeking the attachments we so desire and need. The cycle has now run its course and then repeats.

Changing the Dance

The "Porcupine Dance" is an attempt to handle the tension between two competing drives—attachment wishes and pain avoidance. We want to be close but don't want to be hurt. We seek what relationships provide but shun what relationships all bring in some form—problems. But the dance doesn't resolve the tension, it only perpetuates it. And for some people, it's a dance marathon that lasts a lifetime.

So how can porcupines stop dancing? Or, to ask the question in human terms, how can we be close to people when closeness is certain to bring problems with people? Porcupines get close by relaxing their quills; people get close by solving their people problems—problems that stem from being flawed and imperfect. Closeness to others necessitates solving our problems with others. But our natural tendency is to handle people problems poorly. That's what we will cover next.

 In a Nutshell

We are all driven by two conflicting forces—a drive to attach and a drive to avoid pain. When we attach to others, we have problems with others, which is painful. So we have a dilemma: how to be close to others when closeness involves pain. We become like porcupines whose quills protrude whenever closeness occurs. We want to be close, but we don't want to get poked. It's a tough problem, but one that can be resolved.

For Reflection

1. Name some situations when you've noticed your quills pushing someone away. How have you overcome that? Or have you?

2. Do you think there are ways to be close to others and never be hurt? Why or why not?

3. What events contributed to any reluctance you might have to be close?

4. How has technology (TV, Internet, video games, etc.) helped or hurt in your quest for closeness? How about for others?

5. Can you live happily without close relationships? Why or why not?

Chapter 2

THE CONFLICT TRAP

Life could be wonderful if people would leave you alone.
CHARLIE CHAPLIN

*A meal of bread and water in contented peace
is better than a banquet spiced with quarrels.*
PROVERBS 17:1

When we get close to people, we have problems with people. If we handle those problems well, we'll enjoy closeness. If we don't, we won't. Before exploring how to handle problems well, which we'll do in Sections 2 and 3, we need to look at what happens when they're handled in the way that comes most naturally to us. *Bad conflict* or *conflict trap* describes what occurs when human nature governs the people-problem process. Understanding the dynamics of bad conflict helps us answer a question that people have been asking forever: "Why can't we all just get along?"

Bad Conflict

Obviously *bad conflict* results when people problems are handled poorly. This is what happens if we do nothing to counter our natural inclinations. In fact, it occurs so easily that even animals have their own versions of bad conflict. Handling problems badly requires no thought, no training, no practice. We argue but accomplish nothing. We spend our energy reacting to each other's reactions, leaving the problems unsolved. Bad conflict may also be called the *conflict trap* because it easily ensnares us and, once we fall in, it's hard to exit.

Before we get into a detailed explanation of bad conflict, here are two examples.

Neil and Laura have been married for 22 years. They argue like little children. Laura argues loudly, while Neil simmers in silence, typically withdrawing into a shell whenever the decibel level elevates into the red zone. But when Neil has enough, he erupts viciously. When Neil and Laura argue, their neighbors know it. (In Section 2, I'll explain more about this couple, how they escaped the conflict trap, and how they changed their conflict system from bad to good.)

The second example is the marriage of Patrick and Beth, who are friends of mine. They didn't argue openly but mutilated each other with unspoken hostilities. They practiced the Eleventh Commandment: "If issues arise that causeth conflict, thou shalt keepeth thine mouth shut." They believed that ignoring conflict would make it go away. The less said, the better. When Patrick and Beth argued, their closest friends could easily miss it. The couple reacted to each other's reactions not by attacking, but by withdrawing into silence. Their noiseless battles had the same results as Neil and Laura's—arguing but getting nowhere.

Bad conflict occurs anywhere we find people—on the playground, in families, at work, at school, in the community, in politics, between nations, and even at church. We see it on political talk shows where issues are "debated" between combatants, each one occupying a quadrant of the split screen. One person makes a point while the others roll their eyes or use body language suggesting, *I think you're a Neanderthal.* They interrupt each other, talk over each other, condescend to each other, fail to answer questions, and mischaracterize each other's positions. After three to five minutes of loudly and rudely reacting to each other's reactions, the host thanks them for coming and cuts to a commercial. Though points may be scored, these verbal slugfests are extremely frustrating to watch and generally accomplish nothing.

The following diagram depicts bad conflict (or the conflict trap). Everyone falls into it, but some people seem to establish permanent residences there.

Bad Conflict
The Conflict Trap

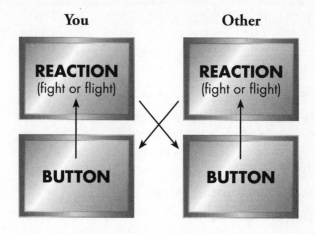

How Does Bad Conflict Happen?

Bad conflict comes about as a result of a natural progression.

Flaws and Differences Become Evident

When we live with or work closely with others, the flaws we spoke about earlier become evident. We also become aware of our differences—different styles, different opinions, different approaches, different preferences, and so on. And the closer the contact, the more likely we are to notice the flaws and differences. We all look better from a distance. That's why it's said, "Fish and company stink after three days" and "Familiarity breeds contempt."

Buttons Get Pushed

When we're in agreement, no problem. But when flaws and differences come into play, buttons get pushed. *Buttons* are places where we feel insecure, weak, particularly sensitized, or easily threatened. We all have them. Buttons are being spoken of when we use phrases such as:

- That's one of my pet peeves.
- He's on my last nerve.
- That really gets next to me.
- She has issues.
- That hit a sore spot.
- That's so insulting.
- She wears her heart on her sleeve.
- That crawls all over me.
- That hurts my feelings.
- He really took offense at that.
- I think I touched a nerve.
- Her wire got tripped.

Types of Buttons

When buttons get pushed, we feel threatened. There are two main types of threats. If I swing a stick at you, I'm threatening you *physically,* and you'll go into self-protective measures. The spoken or unspoken communication is, *I'm going to physically hurt or kill you.* Your brain perceives the threat and certain physiological responses occur such as dry mouth, racing heart, and sweaty palms.

But we can also be threatened *conceptually.*[1] With conceptual threats, the spoken or unspoken communication is, *You're wrong* or *Something is wrong with you.* Being wrong threatens us emotionally every bit as much as a stick threatens us physically, and our brains produce the same physiological responses. Again, conceptual threats are just as real to us as physical threats. In fact, we even use physical language to describe conceptual threats:

- I've been kicked in the gut.
- That was a bitter pill to swallow.
- I've been stabbed in the back.

- He just bit my head off.
- My character has been assassinated.

Gregory Lester sums up this idea very well:

> The world of the conceptual is as dangerous as the physical world. "Sticks and stones can break my bones, but words can never hurt me" is the most precisely inaccurate saying of all time. Words can hurt. Words can kill.[2]

With physical threats, we are fighting to stay alive. With conceptual threats, we are fighting to stay right. Buttons are places of conceptual threat.

Reasons for Buttons

Sometimes we refer to buttons as insecurities—areas where we feel inadequate or fear that something may be wrong with us. All of us have these places, but each person has an individualized set. There are at least four reasons for buttons: our experiences, our brains, our maturity levels, and our convictions.

Our experiences. When we experience an emotional injury, our brains store the pain of that experience in long-term memory, resulting in an area of sensitivity. If something in the present reminds us of the past experience, that button gets pushed. For instance, if every significant relationship in life has ended, getting close to someone becomes associated with getting hurt. Consequently, closeness may push the "abandonment" button.

Our brains. People's brains are wired differently. Two individuals may have equal IQ scores but very different cognitive abilities and traits of temperament. Most people are sensitive about what they perceive to be weak areas, and if we are expected to exercise a strength we don't possess, that button gets pushed. For instance, if we're naturally introverted, being in a setting that requires extraversion may push a "shyness" button.

Our immaturities. We all have gaps between how mature we should be and how mature we actually are. Areas of immaturity create buttons. If life requires us to be mature in one of those areas, our button gets pushed. For instance, if we're in the process of developing assertiveness, being required to assert ourselves may push the "wimpy" button.

Our convictions. Most of us have topics about which we feel strongly. It pushes our "hot button" if someone challenges or disrespects one of those areas. For instance, if we have strongly held political views, a button gets pushed if someone from the opposite end of the political spectrum challenges one of our positions.

Regardless of the reason, buttons are pushed by conceptual threats, which are suggestions of wrongness. If we could somehow monitor the internal dialogues of the people in our examples, we'd hear these thoughts:

- People leave me because something's wrong with me.
- If I were a better person, I wouldn't be so shy.
- My inability to assert myself means that I'm a wimp.
- I'm being told that my views are wrong.

The theme that runs through each of these thoughts is, "There may be something wrong with me." The pain that accompanies that thought elicits a reaction, which is the next step in the progression.

Reactions Occur

If I got in your face, yelled, and repeatedly punched you in the shoulder, you'd probably react by punching me in the nose. Why? Because we're wired to protect ourselves when physical threats occur. When conceptual threats occur, the same thing happens. We react automatically, instinctively, reflexively, without thought or conscious deliberation.

Negative reactions send us into fight or flight mode. When a tiger feels threatened, it goes after its attacker (fight). When a turtle feels threatened, it goes into its shell (flight). Both are reactions to physical threats. When threatened by conceptual attackers, we do the same thing, being like tigers on some occasions and like turtles on others. We attack or withdraw, shout or pout, spew or stew, blow up or shut up.

Fight Reactions

Fight reactions are displayed externally through actions such as yelling and hitting. They are audible and visible. Sometimes 911 gets called when fight reactions occur. Fight reactions are being referred to when these phrases are used:

- going off on someone
- going ballistic
- snapping
- coming unglued
- flying off the handle
- hitting the ceiling
- losing your temper
- losing it
- fighting fire with fire
- letting someone have it
- being at each other's throats

Flight Reactions

Flight reactions are just as real as, but less noticeable than, fight reactions. While fight reactions are externally observable, sometimes flight reactions display themselves subtly. Flight reactions rarely prompt calls to 911 (i.e., "Please send a patrol car, my wife is freezing me out."). Frequently referred to as *conflict avoidance,* some phrases that describe flight reactions are:

- shutting up, shutting down, shutting the person out

- leaving the premises
- changing the subject
- dropping the subject
- sweeping it under the carpet
- going to sleep
- engaging in the "silent treatment" or the "freeze out"
- acting as if the conflict never happened
- going along to get along
- uttering the universal term of resignation, "whatever"
- giving in just to end the argument
- steering clear of potentially contentious subjects
- keeping busy to avoid arguments

The Other Person's Buttons Get Pushed

Whichever type of reaction we display—fight or flight—it pushes the other person's button and elicits his or her reaction, which may repush our button, leading to another reaction, and on and on. And here we are—in a conflict trap, the cycle repeating itself and feeding on itself. Like the wheels of a car spinning in mud, we go "'round and 'round" but never get anyplace. I've often shown the diagram at the beginning of this chapter to couples who view it and say, "That's us. We've been doing that for the last 20 years."

One version of the conflict trap is the loud version, often described using phrases such as blow ups, blow outs, knock down–drag outs, shouting matches, and fighting like cats and dogs. The silent version, where both individuals react by withdrawing, is often referred to when someone says, "You can cut the tension in that room with a knife." No one is arguing openly but the battle is very real.

There is the mixed version where one person is a tiger and the other is a turtle. Or there is the genteel version, where attacks are delivered in sugary-sweet sideways comments accompanied by smiling faces. There are many variations. But whatever the type, living in the conflict trap for long stretches of time is hurtful to the participants.

How Does Bad Conflict Hurt Us?

Bad conflict hurts us in quite a few ways. Let's look at some common ones.

No Problems Are Solved

When we're caught in the conflict trap, all energy goes into button pushing and reacting and none into problem solving. Consequently, the problem that caused the conflict in the first place continues. Trapped couples often say, "We never resolve anything" and "We've been having the same argument for 15 years." They spar for a while, but when the conversation ends nothing's been solved. Their arguments don't reach resolutions; they reach stopping points.

When that happens, many people unwittingly create a mental list of topics to be avoided. *As long as we don't talk about these things,* the thinking goes, *we'll get along just fine.* The phrase used to describe this is "elephants in the living room," as in "There's this elephant in the living room that we keep walking around." Another animal kingdom phrase for the list is "can of worms," as in "Boy, you just don't want to open that can of worms," referring to topics that set off negative reaction cycles when discussed. As time goes on, the list of to-be-avoided topics can become quite lengthy. John Ortberg addresses the detrimental effects of this:

> Marriages can last for decades—sometimes for a lifetime—and look quite pleasant from the outside. Not much conflict, not many storms. But the reality is that the husband and wife are living in pseudocommunity. They talk about the kids or the job or the mortgage, but it doesn't go beneath the surface. They haven't told the truth in years about their loneliness or hurt or anger. Their sexual desires and frustrations go unnamed. They

are disappointed in their marriage and each other, but
neither has the guts to speak frankly and honestly. So
every day they die a little more.[3]

Many people say, "We argue over the silliest things." Small problems result in big arguments when bad conflict is the method used
to solve them. The trouble is not so much with the particular problem as with the system—bad conflict—being used to solve it. That's
why couples build their dream homes, move in, and then divorce. Or
churches split over which color to pick for the carpet. Or adult siblings
no longer speak after an elderly parent dies. In each case, the inability
to solve the problem divided them more than the specific problem
causing the conflict.

Some attempt to avoid people problems by matching themselves
with like-minded others, the assumption being that compatibility
makes problems less frequent or less difficult to resolve. Compatibility
certainly has its place, but *the ability to handle the inevitable incompatibilities is far more important to the success of a relationship.* Some couples,
while remarkably compatible, are trapped in bad conflict because they
don't work through differences. Other couples with limited compatibil-
ities do a great job of resolving differences and have great relationships.
When appearing as a guest on Oprah Winfrey's show, Billy Graham
was asked to explain the secret of his successful and lengthy marriage
to his wife. He replied, "Ruth and I are happily incompatible." Compatibility is desirable, but the ability to resolve differences is essential.
Soul mates are more often developed than discovered.

It Feels Awful

Couples practicing the loud version of the conflict trap often say,
"We just can't live like this." Couples practicing the silent version of the
conflict trap make the same statement: "We just can't live like this."
The silent version is less audible but just as miserable and exhausting.
Bad conflict feels bad, regardless of the type of conflict approach being
practiced.

Think about how it feels to be in a restaurant next to a squabbling couple or in a car with a silently arguing couple. Or maybe you grew up in a family where your parents practiced bad conflict and the atmosphere of the home stayed negatively charged. It feels bad to be in it, but it also feels bad to be around it.

Diminished Hope

Inside the conflict trap, morale is low, pessimism is high, there is no sense of goodwill, and there is little hope for positive change. People caught in the trap often don't like each other and doubt that warm, positive feelings will ever be possible. If there was a gauge that measured emotional warmth, the level would drop a notch with each occurrence of bad conflict, eventually reaching zero. That's why people say, "We love each other, but we're not in love any more" and "I love him, but I don't like him."

At the beginning of this chapter I mentioned Patrick and Beth, who fell into the silent version of the conflict trap. Patrick was attending seminary with the goal of becoming a pastor. From all appearances, they were very compatible and well suited for each other. Yet he and Beth began experiencing struggles shortly after they married. Unlike Neil and Laura, who experienced open hostility and fast-paced bickering, Patrick and Beth withdrew into a frosty world of agonizing silences and unexpressed animosities. They were each deeply hurt by the other's withdrawal, which would then trigger their reactive withdrawals. They became hopelessly ensnared. Finally it got so bad that Patrick prayed this prayer each day:

> Now, Lord, I don't have to tell you how awful my marriage is. It's really bad. I just can't think of any way it could ever improve. And what bothers me the most is that I can't come up with any legitimate way to fix the situation. So, Lord, the only thing I can think of is that you're going to have to take one of us home. Now, I'm not asking you to kill Beth. You can kill me if you want

to. That way I can be in heaven with you, and Beth can marry someone else. So that's my prayer, Lord. Take one of us home. Please bless all the missionaries. Amen.

Sounds goofy, doesn't it? Patrick was requesting a heavenly hit man to end the misery of their situation. He understood that such a request was ridiculous, but he felt that miserable.

Diminished Energy

Bad conflict is exhausting. Like treading water in the ocean, we can do it for a while but not forever. Arguing and getting nowhere will eventually cause us to conclude, "We just can't live like this." Conflict trap participation drains us of energy.

Diminished Trust

Sadly, the problem that brings many couples into my office is a trust violation. One person felt so bad inside the relationship that something outside the relationship offered greater appeal, leading him or her to betray the trust of the relationship.

To work through this problem, we must first define the nature of the violation. Second, we have to see why it happened and change those conditions so that it's not likely to happen again. Almost always, the context in which trust violations occur is some version of bad conflict. The system wasn't working and felt bad, so betraying the trust seemed justifiable. As we'll see later, trust can only be restored when bad conflict conduct is replaced with good conflict conduct.

Relationships Become Alienated

The trap of reacting to each other's reactions feels awful. If we're in a close relationship and the bad conflict process kicks in whenever differences arise, we'll back up from the relationship to avoid the frustration. If we both participate in the distancing process, we develop Ortberg's "dance of the porcupines." Getting close means getting hurt, so distancing is used as a protective barrier. That's why people avoid each other and say, "I'd rather be anywhere but home."

Distancing can occur noticeably or imperceptibly. People often say, "We've drifted apart," as if the drifting was something that happened *to* them. More likely, they've been avoiding the bad feelings of bad conflict by distancing themselves in a thousand little ways over time. In the process, their relationship has become increasingly disconnected, with fewer and fewer common interests. Sadly, many couples, in describing their relationship, say, "We're not living; we're just existing."

It Brings Out Your Worst

Think about how you look and sound when you stub your toe. Not very attractive, is it? For those few seconds, you are being your *reactive* self—the ugly version of yourself. You'd hate to have those images and sounds preserved on videotape.

The self that participates in bad conflict is the reactive self—not the best version of ourselves. In fact, staying involved in bad conflict causes us to become an increasingly worse version of ourselves, resulting in poor judgment, personal stagnation, and physical illness.

Poor Judgment

Pain, both physical and emotional, can distort our perspectives and impair our judgment. When discomfort is high, choices may be shaped less by reason and more by the drive to make the pain stop. That's why it's unwise to make major decisions during times of significant distress. Bad conflict provides a context in which people make foolish decisions, such as having an affair, impulsively resigning from a job, or punishing a child in a way that is harsh and extreme.

Personal Stagnation

None of us reaches adulthood in one piece. There are parts of ourselves that are developmentally younger than our chronological age. In other words, we have "gaps" between how mature we should be and how mature we actually are. Usually we're unaware of our gaps until they become apparent in relationships. Relationships are mirrors in which we catch gap glimpses—reflections of the immature parts of ourselves. If we make use of gap glimpses, we grow. For instance, you may be insensitive…but unaware of your insensitivity, until your spouse reflects back to you that your brashness is causing problems. If you accept the reflection and respond by developing sensitivity, you grow. As we'll see, that's what happens with good conflict. But if bad conflict rules the day, you'll react instead of responding, saying something like, "I'm insensitive? Well, excuse me, oh great bastion of tenderness! Let's talk about your insensitivity." The resulting reactive battle perpetuates your immaturities. While good conflict accelerates your growth, bad conflict stunts it.

Physical Illness

Bad conflict can literally make us sick. Leaving people problems unsolved is stressful, and if we do so repeatedly, the stress we experience is chronic. We're not harmed by short-term elevations of stress, but chronic elevations compromise the immune system and provide a context for various illnesses to develop. For instance, imagine living in a small room for a month with a rattlesnake. Even if the snake never struck at you, your body would be physiologically altered by the end of the month due to the chronic stress of constant exposure to danger for 30 days. When stress goes up and stays up, the immune system weakens and illness is more likely.

Nicholas Hall is a pioneer in the field of psycho-neuro-immunology, which explores the connections between stress and the development of disease. He said,

> In people, impaired memory, coronary arterial disease, increased susceptibility to infection, and autoimmune disorders are all exacerbated by emotional stress. What all the studies point to is the fact that it is not the conflict, but how you respond to the conflict that predicts the health outcome.[4]

The stress generated by bad conflict adversely affects your health. (A diagram depicting bad conflict is located in the Appendix.)

Now, let's look at bad conflict's alternative—good conflict.

Good Conflict

For years Doug used his wife, Debra, as a verbal punching bag. When she finally had all she could take, she moved out. Fortunately, Debra's action served as a wake-up call for Doug, and that's when he came to me for help. He knew he needed to work on himself, but he also hoped to repair the damage he'd inflicted on his marriage. We talked a lot about bad conflict and his contributions to it. His buttons were exceptionally sensitized, his powder-keg overreactions were lightning quick, and he viciously pushed Debra's buttons, using his well-developed verbal skills to slice her to pieces. But now he was ready to find a better way to do conflict. That was music to Debra's ears!

Early on I introduced Doug to this idea: The alternative to bad conflict is not the absence of conflict but *good* conflict. The strife between Doug and Debra couldn't be eliminated, but the system used to deal with it could be changed. This was a new concept to Doug because he'd never seen any good come from conflict. In fact, he and Debra were separated because of it. The term itself, *good conflict,* seemed oxymoronic. How could anything about conflict be good? It sounded a little like saying "good poison ivy." But eventually Doug saw that if he didn't replace the bad conflict system with one that worked, his marriage had little chance of survival. One day, Doug made this remark:

> I understand bad conflict because we've had so much experience with it, and it's really clear in my mind. When I think about it, a million pictures come to mind of us doing it that way. But when I think about good conflict, it's hard for me to get my head around it. I understand it intellectually, and it makes perfectly good sense. But there are no pictures in my head of Debra and I practicing it.

Perhaps you agree with Doug's assessment. If most of your experiences with conflict have been bad, good conflict sounds like an ivory tower concoction that doesn't actually exist in the real world. But let me assure you! It does exist, and many people handle conflict the good way.

What Is Good Conflict?

Bad conflict is bad because nothing good comes from it. Good conflict, on the other hand, has a positive outcome. "Good conflict" may feel bad when we're in the middle of it, but the results are good so it's worth the effort. It enables us to say,

- We argue but we work through our problems.
- We settle things and forget about them.
- We do well with each other despite our differences.
- I'm handling my conflict with that person in the healthiest way possible.
- I don't let that person get to me like I used to.

How Does Good Conflict Happen?

Every winter my son and I go skiing in the mountains of North Carolina. I'm an average skier and not a pretty sight to behold as I descend the slopes, but I can do it. The first year we went, I taught my son to ski. I had never given anyone skiing instructions and struggled to articulate just what to do and how to do it. At one point I said, "Remember, if you do what comes naturally, you'll wipe out. You sometimes have to do the exact opposite of what you think you should, leaning this way when you think you should be leaning that way. If you do that, you'll stay up."

Conflict is like that. If we lean the way that comes naturally, following our intuitive impulses, bad conflict results. If we lean in new ways, making counterintuitive choices, good conflict results. For good conflict to happen, we must *go against the grain* and *intentionally* do certain things to make it happen.

There is a caveat though. There are two groups of people: reasonable and unreasonable. Good conflict methods used with one group won't work with the other, so we must approach them differently.

Good Conflict with Reasonable People

Good conflict among reasonable people requires action in three areas that we'll discuss in Chapters 3 through 5. First, there are five conflict resolution abilities needed for countering our natural inclinations toward bad conflict. I call these *reason muscles* because they can be strengthened with use. We can't flee the trap of bad conflict without using these muscles. Second, there are three places to break the cycle, enabling conflict tensions to de-escalate. We must restrict our buttons, learn to respond rather than react, and refrain from pushing the other person's buttons. Finally, there are five questions that must be answered for conflict problems to be solved.

Good Conflict with Unreasonable People

Good conflict with unreasonable people requires action in the three areas we'll discuss in Chapters 6 through 8. First, we must understand unreasonable people and the methods they use to handle conflict—staging dramas in which they play one of several "good guy" roles. Second, we must understand how to avoid participating in the dramas that only accomplish their purposes when we're enticed into playing our parts. Third, we must establish good boundaries and acknowledge that the relationship will have certain limitations: limited depth, limited value, and limited growth.

How Does Good Conflict with Reasonable People Help Us?

While bad conflict hurts us and should be avoided, good conflict helps us and should be adopted for many reasons.

Problems Are Solved

With bad conflict, problems aren't solved, so the problem and frustration of not being able to fix it are stored in our memory banks. The old frustration then resurfaces in new arguments, which makes solving the new problems even more difficult. We may repeatedly argue about old problems for years. That's when people say, "I can't believe you're still bringing that up." With good conflict, items on the "elephant list"—what topics we're avoiding—can be discussed and laid to rest. And a problem fixed is a problem forgotten. These issues may not be pleasant to discuss, but the pain of avoiding them is greater than the temporary discomfort of discussing and resolving them.

It Feels Positive

While bad conflict feels awful, good conflict produces positive feelings. Again, it may not feel so great when we're in the middle of it, but it feels great to get through it and lay conflict problems to rest. Bad conflict is a relational morale buster while good conflict is a morale booster. There are countless areas good conflict promotes. Here are a few.

Strengthened Hope

Hopeless couples sometimes ask, "Once the feelings have gone, how do we ever get them back?" This question is usually posed after numerous attempts have failed to reignite the emotional flame that flickered out a while back. Often the question presumes a conclusion: There is no way to get them back.

The way to restore good feelings is to shift conflict systems from bad to good. Earlier we discussed the effects of conflict on the "emotional warmth gauge." Bad conflict causes it to drop; good conflict causes it to rise. It's not automatic, but if we want to warm up a cold relationship we must welcome the friction that accompanies good conflict. If we seek good feelings, we're not likely to find them. If we seek good conflict, we'll find it and good feelings are likely to follow because good conflict produces good feelings. The best way to feel hopeful about a relationship is to have good conflict.

By the way, in response to Patrick's request, God didn't kill him or his wife. After several decades, they are still alive, still together, and glad to be so. Through a lot of hard work they shifted conflict systems, and the loving feelings that evaporated rematerialized. Neil and Laura did that too, and I'll share their process and progress in Section 2.

Increased Energy

Conflict is tiring, even if we do it the good way. But by working through and solving a conflict problem, we gain more energy than we expend. It's like exercise. Yes, it takes energy to get up off the couch and go to the gym, but exercising gives us energy. The statement often made after a successful argument is, "It feels so good to have that behind us. I feel like a big weight has been lifted off my chest." Bad conflict depletes energy; but good conflict replenishes it.

Enhanced Trust

Over the years I've worked with many couples trying to survive a marital betrayal. The question "How do we ever get the trust back?" is frequently asked. A big part of that process involves a system upgrade in which we uninstall the old bad conflict system and install a new system of good conflict.

Typically, trust violations occur in the context of relational alienation. Remaining in bad conflict perpetuates the distance and does nothing to restore the trust. Good conflict enables couples to move toward each other and to be transparent—an absolute necessity for trust restoration. Trust results, not from engaging in the "head to head" battles of bad conflict, but from having "heart to heart" conversations that characterize good conflict. The healthier the conflict, the higher the trust. One way to affair-proof a marriage is for good conflict to become the operating system.

Relationships Become Closer

Threatened porcupines keep their distance because being close means getting poked. If we're having bad conflict with someone, we don't want to get close. Instead, we'll use relational geography as a protective buffer. Good conflict, on the other hand, allows our quills to relax so that relational closeness no longer poses a threat. We can let our hair down, relax, trust, be safe, be understood, and be ourselves.

It's been said, "There is no intimacy without conflict." I agree but would make one adjustment: "There is no intimacy without *good* conflict." If conflict is bad, we move away from each other for protection. If conflict is good, we move toward each other and experience the benefits that healthy relationships are supposed to provide.

It Brings Out Your Best: You Grow

Bad conflict brings out our worst, and we become increasingly shoddier versions of ourselves the longer we stay in it. That's because the self that participates in bad conflict is the *reactive* self. But the self that participates in good conflict is the *real* self, and we become increasingly better versions of ourselves over time, especially in these following areas.

Sound Judgment

The escalated, emotionally charged atmosphere of bad conflict clouds our judgment, increasing the danger of making bad choices. In the de-escalated, nonreactive environment of good conflict, we're more likely to make good decisions. Good conflict helps us think straight and choose wisely.

Personal Growth

No one grows in isolation. Relationships are to humans what air, water, and soil are to plants. Without them, we simply don't grow. But for growth to take place, relationships must be healthy, and part of what makes for a healthy relationship is handling conflict in a healthy way. That's good conflict.

In close relationships, our shortcomings clash with those of others, acting much like sandpaper to a rough surface. If the system works well, the abrasiveness we experience, though painful, results in a smoother version of us. Rough edges are knocked off, our immature parts begin to grow, and we become better versions of ourselves. Remember, bad conflict stunts our growth while good conflict accelerates it.

An old Chinese proverb says, "Be not afraid of growing slowly, be afraid of standing still." If we want to grow, we must be involved in relationships that use good conflict methods to resolve differences. And growth makes us happy. William Butler Yeats said,

> Happiness is neither virtue nor pleasure,
> Nor this thing nor that
> But simply growth.
> We are happy when we are growing.[5]

Physical Health

Earlier we discussed how the chronic stress of bad conflict compromises our immune systems, raising the risk for the development of various illnesses. The phrase "I'm sick and tired of all the arguing" can be literally true.

When the good conflict system is used, relational stress decreases. Many studies attest to the beneficial effects of healthy relationships on physical health, and relationships can't be healthy without good conflict. In short, bad conflict makes us sick while good conflict is good for our health.

Now let's look at how good conflict helps us with unreasonable people.

How Does Good Conflict with Unreasonable People Help Us?

Problems Are Restrained

As we'll discuss in Section 3, unreasonable people lack the abilities needed for healthy conflict resolution. We can't solve problems with them like we can with reasonable people, but we can *restrain* the problems in such a way that they no longer dominate the landscape of our lives.

For instance, Mr. Jones had an obnoxious neighbor with an obnoxious dog, who regularly dug up his flowers and made unwelcome deposits in his yard. All efforts to persuade the neighbor to leash his dog failed, and it became clear to Mr. Jones that he was attempting the impossible—trying to reason with an unreasonable person. Finally Mr. Jones put up a fence, which kept the canine terrorist from terrorizing his existence.

In this example, no mutually agreeable resolution was reached because the neighbor's unwillingness to reason made that impossible. But Mr. Jones did find a way to keep the dog out of his yard. The problem was not actually fixed, but a boundary enabled it to be restrained.

You Feel Empowered

With reasonable people, good conflict generates positive feelings because it feels good to work through differences. But with unreasonable people, who lack healthy conflict resolution abilities, good conflict doesn't feel good so much as it feels empowering. Before erecting the fence, Mr. Jones stayed irritated all the time, much of his life being consumed by the situation. After putting up the fence, he had more control over where to devote his time and energy. It's not that he felt good about it, but the fence enabled him to have some power over what was irritating him. Mr. Jones changed his circumstances for the better, despite the fact that his neighbor hadn't changed his mind.

Relationships Can Be Good but Limited

With reasonable people, we can solve conflict problems and get closer. With unreasonable people, the inability to solve conflict problems limits the degree to which we can get close. Consequently, our relationships with unreasonable people may be cordial though more superficial than we'd prefer.

When the fence went up, the dog tensions went down. This enabled Mr. Jones and his neighbor to engage in occasional pleasantries such as talking about the weather. Close friends they would never be, but they could be polite neighbors. Years ago, somebody somewhere was thinking about this and came up with the phrase, "Fences make good neighbors."

Good Conflict Brings Out Your Best

Doing conflict the good way helps us, even when our conflict opponent is an unreasonable person who lacks healthy conflict resolution abilities. Good conflict requires maturity, and the more we do it, the more we grow. Mr. Jones was totally preoccupied with the dog situation, and being at home seemed more like a battleground than a haven. For a while he fantasized about ways to exact revenge, such as redepositing the deposits on the neighbor's porch. All of his natural inclinations pulled him in that direction, but he realized that following those impulses would only bring him down to the neighbor's childish level. The action of putting up the fence accomplished what conversations with the neighbor never could. It was a form of "being the bigger person." By handling it better, Mr. Jones changed for the better.

Mr. Jones' neighbor didn't change. He continued to be his nasty, irascible self. It would be wonderful if good conflict produced positive change for both sides. Unfortunately, the unreasonable person often remains the same, though the effects of his negative qualities are restrained.

In this chapter we've looked at two types of conflict: bad and good. This chart contrasts the effects of these conflict methods.

The Effects of Conflict

Bad Conflict	Good Conflict with Reasonable People	Good Conflict with Unreasonable People
No problems are solved	Problems are solved	Problems are restrained
It feels awful	It feels positive	It feels empowering
Relationships become alienated	Relationships become closer	Relationships can be good but limited
It brings out your worst	It brings out your best You grow	It brings out your best You grow; he or she may not grow

▊ In a Nutshell ▊

Bad conflict should be avoided because nothing good comes from it. Also known as the *conflict trap,* bad conflict is what happens when we get caught reacting to each other's reactions. The results of bad conflict are negative. Good conflict should be adopted because it helps us achieve positive interactions. The methods used to achieve good conflict with reasonable people are different from the methods used with unreasonable people.

▊ For Reflection ▊

1. Take a moment to identify your buttons. Who pushes them most regularly?

2. In what ways do you most often react when your buttons are pushed?

3. Are you a "tiger" or a "turtle" or both?

4. Can you tell when you've pushed someone's buttons? How?

5. Why is compatibility not enough to ensure a happy relationship?

6. How has bad conflict affected your personal growth? Physical health?

7. In what ways (big and small) do you distance from someone close to you because of bad conflict?

8. How are your maturity gaps affecting your relationships?

REASONING WITH THE
REASONABLE

'd just finished explaining the concept of bad conflict to a middle-aged man distressed about the state of his marriage. We talked through the conflict trap diagram discussed in Chapter 2. After a brief pause, he said, "This is exactly what my wife and I have been doing for years. Uh…so where are the off-ramps for this thing?" In the next three chapters we'll look at the off-ramps.

Howard Hendricks observes that couples in conflict have three options: bail out, stick it out, or work it out.[1] Sadly, about half of all couples bail out of marriages. Of the half that stay together, many are simply sticking it out in relationships with limited growth and intimacy. But other couples work it out and spend the rest of their lives cultivating marriages that grow closer and deeper.

What exactly does "work it out" entail? When people solve people problems, how do they do it? In this section we'll take a microscope and examine what happens in the space between a conflict problem arising and a conflict problem being fixed. What takes place in that space is what I call *good conflict*.

When I was in graduate school some of my classmates persuaded me to take up golf. I bought a set of used clubs with a bright red bag for $50 at a yard sale. I wasn't the most fashionable guy on the course, but at least now I could play. I soon discovered that I was an absolute pro at hitting the ball in any direction but straight. This ability came so naturally to me. Seeing how exasperated I was, my wife got me a golf video in which this guy described the mechanics of hitting a straight shot. He explained it well, and it made perfectly good sense. Armed with my newfound knowledge, I took off for the driving range…only to discover that the correct information had failed to correct my shot. I was still hooking and slicing every ball I hit. *Maybe the guy didn't know what he was talking about,* I thought. *Or maybe this is what happens when you pay $50 for a set of clubs.* But after about four buckets of balls, I started hitting the balls straight, just like the guy described. It simply took me a while to correctly and consistently implement the information.

Reading these chapters will be like watching a golf video. The information is correct, but the information alone won't correct a faulty conflict system. That will take practice. Bad conflict comes naturally to us; good conflict doesn't come naturally but becomes second nature through repetition. Many routine tasks such as typing, driving a car, operating a computer, or using the extra features on a cell phone may seem complicated at first, but they become second nature once they're mastered. Good conflict is like that. It's not automatic, but it is achievable. Don't give up!

A real life example is that of a couple who swapped conflict systems—from bad to good. I mentioned them in Chapter 2, Neil and Laura. I'll share more about them over the next three chapters—about how they learned to do conflict the good way. Keep in mind that while this story is about marital conflict, the same principles apply to conflict at work, at school, in church, in parent–child relationships, and any place we interact with people.

The Story of Neil and Laura

Neil and Laura had been married for 22 years and had two boys, ages 19 and 15. Jason was the "good child," giving his parents little trouble and few challenges. The younger son, Kevin, had always been "high maintenance." What to do about Kevin was the starting point for most of Neil and Laura's arguments.

When they first came to my office, I asked them to explain why they sought counseling. They looked at each other and simultaneously said, "You go first," and then sparred over who should take the floor.

Finally Laura said, "We're having a big disagreement over our son, Kevin."

As she was talking, Neil shook his head and made grunting noises.

Laura stopped in mid-sentence, looked at him exasperatedly, and said, "What? What?"

Neil shrugged his shoulders and said, "I didn't say anything. Just make sure you don't conveniently leave out the part about who starts all the arguments."

"You've got to be kidding!" Laura shouted. "You think I start all the arguments?"

"Go ahead with your explanation," said Neil calmly.

At this point, my highly developed powers of perception enabled me to ascertain that this was going to be a really fun session. What follows is the condensed version of what took place over the next hour.

> *Laura:* We've got a decision to make about Kevin going on a Europe trip arranged by his school, but Neil refuses to talk about it.
>
> (Long pause)
>
> *Neil:* We've discussed it. It just doesn't do any good to talk about it. You know where I stand.
>
> *Laura:* That's just it. I don't know where you stand. You've said you don't want him to go, but I'm not sure why.
>
> (Long pause)
>
> *Neil:* I think he's spoiled. He has this entitlement thing going and sending him would only spoil him more.
>
> *Laura* (loudly):
>   All you care about is money. Here we have a chance to give him a once-in-a-lifetime cultural experience, and the only thing on your mind is the almighty dollar. I wish your family mattered to you half as much as your checkbook.

Neil: Uh huh.

Laura (turning to me):
> See, this drives me crazy. He talks to everyone else, especially on the computer, but won't spend time talking just to me.

Neil: I do talk to you but you don't listen…

Laura (interrupting):
> How can I listen when you won't say anything? Oh, you'll talk about work or that boat you worship, but you never spend any time talking just to me.

(Long pause)

Neil (turning to me):
> Laura mentioned worship. She'd have more time to talk if she weren't constantly at church.

Laura (rolling her eyes and looking increasingly exasperated):
> Well, it wouldn't hurt you to darken the door of God's house every now and then either, Mr. Pagan.

Neil: She spends a lot of time at church talking to some guy she met there. I think the whole thing seems really peculiar. And I'm not the only one who thinks it's strange either.

Laura (looking like she could explode):
> Oh, so you think I'm having some kind of affair, do you? Tell us, will you please, about your latest chatroom honey.

(Long pause)

Neil (after I prompted him to talk):
> That self-righteous tone of hers reminds me so much of her mother, I could just throw up.

Laura: It's not like your mother was June Cleaver, you know.

Neil: My mother was always incredibly patient with you, especially when she saw you spoiling the kids rotten.

Laura: Well, it seems like some of that "patience," as you call it, would have rubbed off on her son. And by the way, you won the Absent Father Award, so don't lay all that poor parenting stuff on me.

By now I'm thinking, *Let's see, where did this argument start? We might have to employ an archeologist to unearth the original issue that got buried beneath this avalanche of topics.*

Clearly Neil and Laura were engaged in bad conflict. She was "a tiger" who reacted by attacking, and he was "a turtle" who reacted by withdrawing. His turtle reactions pushed her buttons resulting in tiger reactions, which further pushed his buttons, resulting in turtle reactions. They were trapped. They could never solve a Kevin problem—or any other problem for that matter. Not only did it feel bad to them, but it felt bad to me just being in the same room while they slugged it out.

Like many couples who seek counseling, Neil and Laura were unable to clearly articulate exactly what they hoped to gain by coming. In one sense they were looking for a judge to determine which one was right. In other senses they wanted a doctor to cure their illness, a teacher who could impart some missing information, and a policeman to keep their arguments from getting out of hand. But I determined, instead, to be like a computer guru and help them uninstall their bad conflict system and install a good conflict system.

Their reason for being in my office, as I saw it, was not their difference of opinion about Kevin's trip. Their problem was that they had no system for solving the Kevin problem—or any other problem. Changing the conflict system from bad to good needed to be our focus. Instead of attacking each other, they needed to join forces and attack their malfunctioning conflict system.

Transitioning from bad conflict to good conflict is easier to talk about than it is to do. Good conflict is achievable, but like I pointed out earlier, it's not automatic. I knew that if Neil and Laura were to succeed, they would have to approach the process with different attitudes.

Deliberateness

Some couples come into my office with an *information deficit.* They genuinely lack the knowledge of how to do anything constructive to fix the relationship. Some have a *success deficit,* having unsuccessfully attempted an array of fixes. They've read the latest 10 books on how to make relationships better using certain "skills and drills," how to live with a partner from a different planet, how to speak a different relationship language, or how to avoid playing out their family of origin dynamics. They've attended weekend events, some of which promised a marital cure before leaving on Sunday. They're now demoralized and enter counseling with an understandable degree of skepticism. In some cases, one or both partners has a *motivation deficit,* having adopted a stance of pessimistic resignation. *Why should we put any effort into this? It won't work,* the thinking goes. Some of these people are searching for a coroner to sign the relational death certificate, which declares the marriage officially beyond repair. Neil and Laura had a combination of deficits. They didn't know much, but their few repair attempts had failed miserably. Their expectations of counseling were low. They saw it as something they "ought to do to try to make it work."

Neil and Laura were low on optimism, but that's not a prerequisite for success. More than optimism, they needed deliberateness. Self-fulfilling prophecy has a lot of power. Without the willingness and determination to roll up their sleeves and work, their efforts would likely be sabotaged by small expectations.

Humor

Achieving good conflict requires deliberateness, but serious work requires humor. In the old TV show *MASH,* the doctors and nurses learned to laugh to cope with the daily grimness of piecing back together men who'd been mutilated on the field of battle. Conflict involves emotions, many of them uncomfortable. If we can't find ways to interject some levity, we'll probably avoid conflict to escape the discomfort.

President Ronald Reagan and Speaker of the House Tip O'Neill were fierce political opponents. When it came to philosophy of government, they shared very little ideological common ground. Yet, whenever possible, they met at the end of the day, had a couple of drinks, and told funny stories. They enjoyed each other's presence despite their greatly divergent political views.

Neil and Laura would more likely stick with the process if they could find ways to lighten up. They needed to laugh with each other, to laugh at themselves, and to not take everything so seriously. Doing so would de-escalate the conflict tensions and increase the likelihood of success.

Realism

While bad conflict is easy to achieve, good conflict doesn't come easy. As systems go, good conflict has more moving parts and is more likely, therefore, to break down. Inevitably, something won't go as planned. One person will be more determined than the other, it won't go as fast as we'd like, it will be more complicated than we thought, or old patterns will be more ingrained than we imagined. If our expectations are unrealistic, we'll become discouraged and give up easily, declaring, "I knew this wouldn't work."

Realism is the healthy balance between two unhealthy extremes: pessimism and idealism. Neil and Laura were already pessimistic based upon their poor track record of success. But I encouraged them to also avoid idealistic expectations of a magical, quick fix. Comedian Steven Wright said, "I have a microwave fireplace. I can lie down in front of the fire for an evening in eight minutes." There are no microwave solutions for problems that have been stewing in the Crock-Pot for many years.

Mutuality

The cycle of bad conflict was energized by fuel from both Neil and Laura. Laura pushed buttons by yelling. Neil pushed buttons by withdrawing. To change the system, both of them would need to change their ways. Just as it takes two wings to fly an airplane, when two reasonable people are involved, the participation of both sides is required for good conflict to be achieved. The greater the mutuality of involvement, the better the chances of success.

Neil and Laura would have to fight a very natural tendency called *contingent behavior change:* "I'll change my ways if you change yours. If I don't see it happening over there, it won't be happening over here." Instead, both needed to adopt *this* stance: "I'll change my part whether or not you change yours." Their marital problems were not the 100 percent responsibility of either one, but each one had to assume 100 percent of the responsibility for his or her contributions to the marital problems.

As we look at what's involved in *good conflict with reasonable people* over the next three chapters, I'll explain how Neil and Laura implemented good conflict principles. In Chapter 3, we'll look at how to exercise our "reason muscles," the ones we need for handling personal wrongness. Chapter 4 will discuss ways to escape the trap of bad conflict. In Chapter 5, we'll examine how to solve the problems causing the conflict. (A diagram depicting good conflict with reasonable people is found in the Appendix.)

Chapter 3

FLEXING THE MUSCLES

Criticism may not be agreeable, but it is necessary. It fulfills the same function as pain in the human body. It calls attention to the state of things.

WINSTON CHURCHILL

A quiet rebuke to a person of good sense does more than a whack on the head of a fool.

PROVERBS 17:10

Neil and Laura had grown-up bodies but they argued like children. If "Good Conflict Camp" existed, I might've dispatched the camp van to my office during their first visit to pick them up. "When you get to camp," I would have explained to the driver, "Tell the head counselor that these folks need stronger 'reason muscles.' He'll know what I'm talking about."

Let me explain *reason muscles*. Nobody likes being wrong, a distinct possibility when arguments occur. Arguments are full of conceptual threats, which convey one of the following ideas: "I'm right and you're wrong," "Something about you is wrong," or "Something is wrong with you." These threats push buttons, and our every impulse is to react, which keeps the cycle of bad conflict energized. It takes a lot of strength to handle being wrong. "Reason muscles" enable us to do the right thing with wrongness. They enable us to be reasonable or reason *able*. Without them, we can neither escape the conflict trap nor solve the problems causing the conflict.

As we look at the five "reason muscles," you'll discover how to make yours stronger. You'll also find out what Neil and Laura did to strengthen their muscles—even though they didn't actually go to camp.

The Humility Muscle

Humility is the ability to acknowledge potential personal wrongness. Using this muscle enables us to allow for the possibility that we could be wrong. Not using it brings about an arrogant insistence that it's simply not possible for the wrongness to be on our side. Arguments between people with weak humility muscles don't go well. They engage in "rightness battles," in which the stance of both sides is "I'm right. You're wrong. End of discussion." The button-pushing effect of that stance fuels the reactive cycle and conflict tensions increasingly escalate. Children usually argue this way, and many adults display their own variations. Battle lines are drawn and conversations grind to a halt.

Using the humility muscle enables us to adopt the posture, "I could be wrong, you could be right, let's talk." Simply taking this stance has a de-escalating effect on the conflict tension and opens the way for productive discussions, which allows differences to be aired and worked through. Again, *no one does this naturally. It's learned behavior.* Good conflict comes about as a result of exercising this muscle.

Humility Muscle Exercises

Acknowledge the possibility. This exercise takes place inside our heads and the internal dialogue sounds something like this.

> As much as I hate to admit it, I'm not omniscient. It's possible that the other person sees something I don't. I think I'm right here, but I need to concede the possibility that I could be wrong. Sure, it will hurt if I find out I'm wrong, but I need to remember that truth is more important than being right.

Admit the possibility. This is the external version of the internal exercise just described. We've thought it, and now we say it. Our admission to the other person may be as uncomplicated as "Maybe I'm wrong here" or "You could be right." It's important not to confuse this stance with surrender. We're not admitting we *are* wrong, simply that we *could be* wrong.

Doing this has two effects. First, whenever we verbalize the possibility of wrongness, our humility muscle gets a little stronger. Second, the other person becomes less defensive. When defenses go down, dialogue opens up.

When Neil and Laura Exercised Their Humility Muscles

Not much humility was detected at Neil and Laura's first counseling session. Neil was a quietly reluctant participant, figuring that whatever we discussed had already been said a thousand times so what was the point of further discussion. Laura was quite shrill, attempting to bludgeon Neil into conversations about Kevin's trip, as well as myriad other unresolved issues. She believed our sessions would give her the forum to do so. In different ways, the assumption of each was "I'm right so you must be wrong."

One of our first tasks involved limiting the session focus to just one problem. The one we picked was their difference of opinion about Kevin's Europe trip. Laura thought he should go; Neil did not. Laura had good reasons for her preference, but so did Neil. As long as they stayed entrenched inside their positions of exclusive rightness, they would be defensive and tensions would remain escalated, making further discussion fruitless. Both of them had to personally wrestle with this question: "Which is more important to me—to have a solution to this problem or to be right?"

Opting for a solution over rightness opened communication channels, and tensions de-escalated a little when each became willing to verbalize the potential rightness of the other's position. They didn't do this easily. At first it was like a child saying "I'm sorry." The tone suggested, "I'm only saying this because I'm being made to, but I'm really not sorry at all."

Initially Laura "the tiger" reacted to my suggestion by roaring, "Oh, so I'm just supposed to give in and say he's right about everything?"

"No, you don't have to say he is right...only that he *could* be right," I explained. "And that you're willing to *consider* his position. That's all. And he needs to do the same for you."

Reluctantly, but eventually in a way that was genuine, each adopted this stance. Lack of humility had shut the discussion down. Exercising humility opened it up.

The Awareness Muscle

As previously stated, we all have gaps between how mature we should be and how mature we actually are, between what we should do and what we actually do. We may be unaware of some of them though. Unobserved gaps are called *blind spots,* weak places noticed by others but not by ourselves. Our *awareness muscle* enables us to have *gap glimpses,* to step back and see our blind spots so we can see the good and bad parts of ourselves and address any problem areas. While humility enables us to acknowledge *potential* wrongness, awareness enables us to observe *actual* wrongness. If this muscle is weak, we'll see where we're right but remain oblivious to the places where we're wrong. Two examples illustrate the function of the awareness muscle: *the press box* and *the mirror.*

When we watch football games and see quarterbacks talking on the phone, they're talking to coaches in the press box. The coach sees things from up there that the quarterback can't see from his horizontal perspective. The coach can tell the quarterback why the last series of plays produced a touchdown or why he was just smeared for a 22-yard loss. If the quarterback makes use of the coach's input, of the coach's perspective, he can be more effective on the field. We all have *press boxes* that enable us to step outside of ourselves and make big-picture self-observations. Staying in communication with our press box enables us to make adjustments so that our faults will cause fewer problems. If we don't stay in touch, we won't see our flaws or the problems they cause. And if neither person in the conflict gains press box perspective, the argument becomes very confusing.

The second illustration is that of a *mirror*. Suppose you're eating at a restaurant. You go to the restroom and, in the mirror, observe that your hair looks nice but you have a big glob of spinach on your teeth. The mirror provided feedback concerning what's right and wrong about you. Relationships are like mirrors in which we catch reflections of our strengths and weaknesses. Our awareness muscle enables us to observe our errors so that necessary corrections can be made.

Awareness Muscle Exercises

Welcome press box feedback. The coach in the press box is not a cheerleader but a truth-teller, and the truth helps the quarterback be more effective. We all need a few people in our lives who are willing to tell us the truth, to give us honest feedback on what we're like and how we come across. We need to exercise our willingness to hear the comfortable and uncomfortable parts of their analysis. As we study ourselves, we need to ask:

- What are my areas of immaturity?
- What are my strengths?
- What pushes my buttons?
- When my buttons get pushed, how do I tend to react?
- What is the effect of my reactions on others?
- In what ways do I push their buttons?
- What can I learn about myself by observing their reactions to me?

Look in the mirror. We use mirrors to help ourselves look good and to correct what looks bad. Like press box coaches, mirrors tell us the truth, which is often uncomfortable even though it's helpful. Close relationships are like full-length mirrors in which we can catch reflections of what's good and bad about us. We all have positives and negatives but may be unaware of them until they affect those that are close to us. Our best and worst qualities become apparent to us in up-close, personal relationships. So if we want to know and understand ourselves better—our good parts and our bad parts—we should watch for how those qualities show up in our closest connections.

When Neil and Laura Exercised Their Awareness Muscles

Neil and Laura both had gaps (blind spots) that adversely affected the process of conflict resolution. Laura had a preachy, holier-than-thou manner that manifested itself through statements such as, "Well, it wouldn't hurt you to darken the door of God's house every now and then either, Mr. Pagan." Neil typically reacted by becoming a turtle or by occasionally becoming a snapping turtle and retaliating through retorts such as, "That self-righteous tone of hers reminds me so much of her mother, I could just throw up." This reaction on Neil's side pushed buttons on Laura's side, and the cycle continued. At that point, the argument became more about scoring points than solving the problem, which had long since gotten lost in the confusion of battle. Other blind spots on both sides added to the mayhem.

Actually, Laura was sometimes aware of her self-righteous tone and had every intention of using it as a weapon, hoping it would shame Neil into action. What she failed to see, however, was that using it had precisely the opposite effect. Typically Neil would miss the point she was trying to make and, instead, make her tone and manner of delivery the new topic of discussion. Laura wasn't particularly thrilled with this insight, but it was revealing when Neil said,

> When I hear that tone, I find myself recoiling. It's like I punch the mute button so I don't have to hear anything else you say. And I'm sure that frustrates you. For future reference, it will be easier for me to actually pay attention to what you're saying if you'll drop the sarcasm.

Like looking in a mirror, Laura didn't like what had been revealed but made use of the reflection to make corrections. Neil did the same thing. With those corrections being made, they were better able to stay on task and devote their conversational energy to actual problem solving.

The Responsibility Muscle

The third muscle needed to handle wrongness well is *responsibility*. The awareness muscle enables us to observe our gaps or personal shortcomings. The *responsibility muscle* enables us to be bothered by the awareness. This is sometimes referred to as having a *conscience*. We have gap glimpses, they bother us, and we accept responsibility for them. This doesn't mean we take 100 percent responsibility for the conflict, unless that's accurate. It does mean we take 100 percent of the responsibility for *our* particular contributions to the conflict. When the responsibility muscle is used, the stance is, "It bothers me when I'm wrong." We see our wrongness and cringe. If personal wrongness doesn't bother us, we'll do nothing to correct it. *The responsibility muscle is a necessary prerequisite for change.*

Han Solo, the impetuous anti-hero in *Star Wars,* always said "It's not my fault" whenever something went wrong. When people with weak responsibility muscles argue, they play the "blame game," absolving themselves of responsibility and attributing exclusive blame to the other side. When this strategy inevitably fails, conversations end with no resolution to the conflict.

Responsibility Muscle Exercises

Admit faults. When we become aware of a gap and it bothers us, the most helpful thing to do is take responsibility for it and admit it. "Confession is good for the soul." It's good for us personally, and it also helps conflict move in a good direction. Nothing about this comes naturally but, when we do it, conflict tensions de-escalate.

An important part of admitting our faults involves apologizing for hurtful words or actions. We all resisted doing this as kids, and it doesn't get any easier as adults unless we work at it. Here are some do's and don'ts regarding apologies:

- Do take 100 percent responsibility for your errors. Politicians are often advised to publicly acknowledge errors since people tolerate confession better than evasion. Don't take 100 percent responsibility for all the problem unless that's true.

- Do take the initiative to apologize. Don't wait until you're asked for an apology. It won't mean as much if you do.

- Do apologize for specific offenses (i.e., for wrongly drawing conclusions, for inappropriate reactions, for harsh delivery). Name the particular wrongdoing. Don't apologize for generalities. Specific apologies communicate that you understand the offense. Nonspecific apologies communicate that you're just going through the motions.

- Do apologize sincerely. Examples of insincere apologies are: "If it will make you feel better, I'm sorry" or "I'm sorry you took it that way" or "I'm sorry" (expressed loudly and exasperatedly) or "OK, you're right, you're right, it's all my fault." Note: When we are on the receiving end of an apology, it's important to accept the apology and express appreciation for the other person's willingness to apologize. Avoid minimizing comments such as "Don't worry about it" or "Forget it." It's more helpful to say, "I accept your apology."

Request forgiveness. It's one thing to apologize for the offense but another thing to say, "Will you forgive me?" Not only does this exercise the responsibility muscle but also the humility muscle. It's humbling to request forgiveness.

When Neil and Laura Exercised Their Responsibility Muscles

Neil gave Laura feedback about her self-righteous tone. It stung her, but she was able to accept it and to appreciate her tone's negative effect on the conflict process. The next step for Laura felt risky. She knew she needed to admit her fault and request forgiveness, but nothing inside of her wanted to step across that line. Mustering up her courage and going against her grain, she said, "I know it doesn't help us when I use sarcasm. It's an old habit, and I'll work on it. I apologize for calling you 'Mr. Pagan.' Will you forgive me?"

Laura braced for Neil's reply, fearing he would say, "Well, well, well, it's about time. So you're finally admitting that you do cause all the arguments. That's great. Thanks." Instead he said, "I appreciate you saying that and, yes, I forgive you. I can get pretty sarcastic myself at times so I'll watch my tone too. Thanks."

Admitting faults, requesting forgiveness, and extending forgiveness all had a de-escalating effect on the conflict tension. They had to keep doing this on an as-needed basis, which was pretty often.

The Empathy Muscle

Webster defines *empathy* as "the capacity for participating in another's feelings or ideas." If we are empathic, we seek to understand the other person. We consider the impact of our words and actions and allow that understanding to shape our behavior. With empathy, it bothers us if something we do or say causes pain for another person. Empathy is what compels parents who are disciplining their children to say, "This is going to hurt me more than it hurts you."

When empathy is lacking, people argue in a way that inflicts deliberate injuries, hoping to score points by lobbing emotional grenades into each other's laps. The relationship feels unsafe, the participants feel misunderstood, there is no working through conflict problems, and the pain of harsh words and hurtful actions gets remembered for a long time. Empathy-deficient relationships are characterized by "head to head" confrontations, not by "heart to heart" conversations. Arguments typically end only because continuing them is so painful.

Empathy Muscle Exercises

Understand. In *Seven Habits of Highly Successful People,* Stephen Covey says that we should "seek first to understand, then to be understood."[1] Understanding is often referred to as "being on the same page" with someone. One of the best things in life is to be deeply understood by someone who matters to us. Swiss psychiatrist Paul Tournier said,

> How beautiful, how grand and liberating this experience is, when couples so learn to help each other. It is impossible to overemphasize the immense need [people] have to be really listened to, to be taken seriously, to be understood…No one can develop freely in this world and find full life without feeling understood by at least one person.[2]

On the other hand, one of the worst things in life is to be misunderstood:

- for someone to repeatedly miss our point
- for someone to be convinced that he or she has us figured out, but we know he or she is dead wrong
- for someone to put us into a "box" from which we are not allowed to escape
- for someone to put words in our mouths

When someone we care about fails to understand us, the hurt we experience leads to isolation and loneliness. If we live with those people, we're left feeling alone within the walls of our own homes.

With our *empathy muscle,* our objective is to convince the other person that we understand, and that we know it's vital to keep pursuing understanding until we reach our goal. Conflict tensions de-escalate when each person observes the other trying to understand. How do we communicate this?

- We let the other person know that understanding is important to us by statements such as, "I'm not understanding your
point, but I want to. Bear with me here because it's important
for me to get what you're saying."

- We become ruthless in our pursuit of understanding by not
giving up if we don't get it…even after it's been explained
to us again. We need to ask more questions or say, "I'm not
trying to be difficult, but I'm still not following you. Explain
that to me again because I really want us to be on the same
page." Don't get discouraged if it takes several repetitions.

- We verbalize our understanding and ask for feedback. It
helps when we say, "OK, correct me if I'm wrong, but here's
my understanding of what you're saying (and then share it).
Is that accurate? Am I understanding you correctly?" This
invites the other person to clear up any misinterpretation.

- We listen well. Frasier Crane, the self-absorbed psychiatrist on
the TV show *Frasier* was once asked, "How do you listen to
people all day long?" He pompously replied, "Oh, good God
man, I don't listen!" We all need to listen and to be listened to
because without it, there can be no understanding. In order
to listen well, we must:

  Ask questions. Questions say, "It's important for me to
  understand what you're saying."

  Pause before speaking. Have you ever had this experience?
  You're talking to someone who is anxiously waiting for
  you to finish so he can say his piece. Your conclusion?
  "He's not listening to a word I'm saying." Pausing before
  speaking lets us assimilate what's being said and communicates that we're giving fair consideration to the other
  person's views.

  Avoid interrupting. People hate being interrupted. The
  best way to understand the other person is to avoid

interrupting, even if we disagree with what's being said. Interrupting says, "I already understand what you're saying. Now it's time for you to hear my side."

Listen with body language. It's extremely frustrating to talk with someone who looks and sounds like a statue while we're talking. Head nods, verbal feedback, and eye contact all communicate that we're giving attention to what's being said.

The next empathy muscle exercise, validating, helps the other person feel understood.

Validate. The mission of Apollo 13 (1970) had to be drastically altered due to an onboard explosion that occurred en route to the moon. Lunar landing plans were discarded and replaced with rescue plans for returning the astronauts to Earth. In the movie *Apollo 13,* mission control engineers radioed the astronauts that landing on the moon was no longer possible and waited for the reply "Copy that," which means "we've received your message and understand it." After a long period of silence, the flight director said impatiently, "Did they copy that?" Finally the astronauts dejectedly replied, "Roger, Houston, we copy that."

When we validate someone, we are saying, "Copy that," which means "I see your point and understand it." Validation lets the other person know we understand the content of what's being said or the emotional experience of being in their place. Examples of validating comments are:

- I see your point.
- I can understand how you might see it that way.
- I see what you're saying.
- It makes sense to me that you'd feel the way you do.
- I can understand that.
- Most anyone in your situation would feel like that.

Examples of invalidating comments are:

- Well, that's stupid.
- You shouldn't feel like that.
- That's ridiculous.
- Yeah, sure, whatever you say.
- Silence (no comment at all).

Validation is different than agreement. Agreement affirms rightness while validation communicates *understanding*. We can disagree with a person and still validate him or her. We're saying, "I may not see this the way you do, but I can understand how you might see it this way."

Invalidation occurs when we try to counter emotion with reason through statements such as, "Don't let that bother you" or "Isn't it about time for you to get past that?" or "Get over it." Providing reasons why a person shouldn't feel something is usually invalidating and leaves them feeling misunderstood and angry. For example, just before Penny and I married, we were attending a conference with people like us—twentysomethings. Her insecurities at the time emerged, causing her to exclaim, "Every girl here is prettier than me. I feel so ugly." Attempting an emotional rescue, I heroically took her by the shoulders, looked her in the eyes, and said, "Now listen to me. You are not unattractive. You're beautiful. Do you understand me?" I learned an important lesson: Reason often fails to counter emotion. Much to my surprise, I learned that my comments didn't help at all and made her feel invalidated. I was lucky that day. Penny graciously spared my life. I'm pretty sure that was the last time I made that particular mistake.

Finally, validation can be communicated in ways other than words. When I was growing up my grandmother had a housekeeper named China London, whom we called Chiny for short. She worked for my grandmother for 40 years and was deeply loved by everyone in the extended family. She was a wonderful person who consistently exuded warmth and grace. Being the youngest of all the cousins, I was the one most likely to be interrupted and talked over during conversations at family gatherings. It was exasperating and no one ever noticed—except Chiny. Whenever I would come close to bursting with frustration, she would catch my eye and wink. She never said a word, and we never had a conversation about it, but I felt validated. Chiny was saying to me, "I see what's happening and understand how frustrated you must be. I get it. Copy that." In a nonverbal way she provided me with much-appreciated validation.

When Neil and Laura Exercised Their Empathy Muscles

One of the by-products of Neil and Laura's extended time in the conflict trap was that they had become empathy deficient. The hurtful methods each used to make points or score points triggered vicious retaliatory reactions.

Their most obvious disagreement—among the myriad issues—was their difference of opinion over Kevin's Europe trip. Not exercising empathy, neither felt understood by the other. Consequently they battled over whose opinion had the greater validity. They were stuck in the mud and getting nowhere. They got a little less stuck when they took turns really listening to and understanding each other's reasons for the preference chosen. Laura found out that Neil wasn't just concerned about money. He felt strongly that giving Kevin the trip would reinforce an immature character pattern—his sense of entitlement. Neil found out that Laura wasn't trying to spoil Kevin. She wanted him to have enriching experiences that don't come along very often in life. She felt Kevin would be a better person if he went on the trip.

Once they realized that both opinions had validity, they were less prone to argue over which one was right. Each felt validated by statements such as, "I still disagree, but I can understand why you see it the way you do. That makes sense." Being misunderstood had felt awful, and using their empathy muscles allowed for understanding, which decharged the negative atmosphere inside their home.

The Reliability Muscle

The last muscle needed for handling personal wrongness is the *reliability muscle,* which enables us to correct ourselves. A reasonable person observes his flaws, is bothered by them, and determines to correct them, the stance being, "When I'm wrong, I'll change." Reliability means that *actions follow statements of intent and that what we do is consistent with what we say.* Hence the truism, "Actions speak louder than words." Actions are the external evidence that something has changed internally. When people lack reliability muscles, they may see their faults but not make changes. Comprehension without correction is demoralizing, leading people to say, "What's the point in arguing? Nothing ever changes." As a result, conflict is avoided and problems remain unsolved.

Three good things result from using the reliability muscle. First, using it provides hope and encouragement. When people actually change how they deal with each other, a sense of optimism replaces the pessimism that pervades the relationship.

Second, problems can be forgotten. If something evokes strong emotions, we remember it. Otherwise it gets forgotten, having never been stored in long-term memory. For instance, I don't remember most hamburgers I've eaten except one—the one containing a screw. That was way back in the 1970s. I had strong emotions about that particular hamburger: shock, anger, and then some humor. Had the only ingredients been meat, bread, mayonnaise, cheese, and pickles, I would've forgotten it. But my feelings about the screw made it memorable. Unsolved problems evoke strong emotions: frustration, anger, exasperation, and resentment. If a conflict conversation ends with the problem unsolved, the emotions of that experience cause the problem to get stored in long-term memory. That's why old problems resurface in new arguments, leading someone to say, "You've got a memory like an elephant. I can't believe you're bringing up something that happened 10 years ago." But if the problem is solved, as evidenced by changes in behavior, it gets forgotten and won't likely show up in later arguments. Problems fixed are problems forgotten.

Third, trust is cultivated. People trapped in bad conflict often say, "I have no hope that anything will ever change." Why? Because present actions are repetitions of past patterns. But trust is cultivated when current behaviors that demonstrate observable changes from the patterns of the past continue.

Reliability Muscle Exercises

Target the correction. Let's say you have a gap glimpse, it bothers you, and you decide to correct it. What specifically are you going to correct? How will your change look and sound after it's made? If your answers to these questions are vague, change won't likely occur. The targeted correction needs to be concrete and specific. For instance, vague promises such as "I'll be nicer" or "I'll do better" are less likely to bring about change than specific behavioral commitments such as "I'll stop interrupting you" or "I'll quit throwing sarcastic jabs."

Debrief vs. rehash. When conflict problems aren't solved, they are likely to be rehashed later. *Rehashing* is refighting the argument, reenacting the battle, using the same bad conflict methods employed the first 18 times it was fought. Participants feel awful because when the rehash is over, there's no solution to the problem this time either. Despite the fact that rehashing accomplishes nothing, many people oddly seem to find recreational pleasure in it.

A better option is *debriefing,* which focuses on the process of fixing the problem. Debriefing occurs when we retrospectively analyze the argument with an eye toward making future corrections. Debriefing is what athletes do when they study game films to improve performance in later contests. They're asking, "What did we do wrong, what did we do right, and what do we need to work on?" Similarly, debriefing conversations involve asking and answering two questions:

- What did we do right and wrong in that argument?
- For future reference, what should we do differently?

Debriefing conversations should be kept relatively short. The focus is on learning from past mistakes and correcting them in the future. With debriefing, we do it, learn from it, and move on. It's best to "glance at the past and gaze at the future."

When Neil and Laura Exercised Their Reliability Muscles

After hearing the description of bad conflict, Neil and Laura agreed that Laura was "the tiger" in the relationship and Neil was "the turtle." She was just as offended by his silent withdrawals as he was by her shrill attacks. Neil was bothered by this realization and determined to become less of a turtle. Here's the internal dialogue that typically coursed through his brain when he and Laura argued,

> OK, we're at it again. The best thing you can do right now is keep your mouth closed until she shuts up and quits her yammering. Oops, you almost slipped up and said something. Good job, Neil. Just hold on a little longer, and she'll finally throw in the towel. Yak, yak, yak, yak, yak. Is she ever going to stop? There she goes. Silence, oh wonderful silence. Now all I have to do is let a little time go by and change the subject to something more pleasant. It'll be like this fight never happened, and we can get back to normal living. I wonder what's for supper.

Neil became aware that hunkering down until the storm blew past was his major contribution to the conflict trap. At first his dedication to change was stated so globally that it failed to provide much encouragement. When he said, "I know I shouldn't do that. I'll try to talk more," Laura wasn't blown away with optimism. In fact, she thought,

Yeah, right. I'll believe that when I hear it. With some prodding, Neil expressed his commitment in more concrete terms by saying,

> I understand that when we argue I go silent, and that's really frustrating to you. I need to stop that, so this is what I'll do. When I catch myself doing it, I'll say to you, "Here's one of those times when I tend to shut down and stop talking. So I'll listen to your point right now and try to comment on it. If I don't have anything to say, I'll think about it and give you some feedback in about 10 minutes." If there are times when I seem particularly silent, I want you to ask me, "Are you shutting me out right now?" That will call my attention to it if I haven't noticed. Hopefully, this will help, and if it doesn't work, we'll try something else.

Stating his commitment in specific terms gave Laura a greater sense of encouragement. To be honest, the change process was a little ragged, requiring them to make adjustments when things didn't work out quite the way they envisioned. But they understood that plans conceived in ivory towers like my office have to be altered when the need for change becomes evident.

The table on the next page summarizes the muscles needed for handling personal wrongness, the results of disuse, and ways to exercise them.

In a Nutshell

When we fail to use our reasoning muscles, we are destined to fall back into the trap of bad conflict. Without the use of these muscles, conflict conversations conclude prematurely, leaving the conflict problems unsolved. Reasoning muscles get stronger through exercise.

Handling Personal Wrongness

Reason Muscle	Results of Disuse	Muscle Exercises
Humility The ability to acknowledge potential personal wrongness	Arguments degenerate into "rightness" battles	**Learn to** Acknowledge the possibility, admit the possibility
Awareness The ability to observe actual personal wrongness	Arguments are confusing	**Learn to** Welcome press box feedback, look in the mirror
Responsibility The ability to be bothered by personal wrongness	Both people blame each other for the problems	**Learn to** Admit faults, request forgiveness
Empathy The ability to be bothered if your personal wrongness hurts others	Words and actions are intended to hurt	**Learn to** Understand, validate
Reliability The ability to correct personal wrongness	Nothing changes because neither person sees anything to correct	**Learn to** Target the correction, debrief instead of rehash

For Reflection

1. How important is "being right" to you? How has this hindered problem-solving in your relationships?

2. How do you feel when you become aware of a "maturity gap" and its effects on others? What do you do?

3. Who usually pushes your buttons? Whose buttons do you push?

4. Who tells you the truth?

5. Define *empathy*.

6. Why is it important to pursue understanding?

7. What is the difference between *agreement* and *validation*?

8. Why is it important to be specific when planning a change regarding a "maturity gap"?

9. How is debriefing helpful? Why is rehashing nonproductive?

Chapter 4

FLEEING THE TRAP

When I'm getting ready to reason with a man,
I spend one third of my time thinking about myself
and what I'm going to say,
and two thirds of my time thinking about him
and what he is going to say.
ABRAHAM LINCOLN

A gentle response defuses anger,
but a sharp tongue kindles a temper-fire.
PROVERBS 15:1

W hen I was in graduate school in Oregon, my friends and I
would go skiing on occasion. During one of our trips I formulated the following theory: "You should be able to ski down any hill, regardless of the level of difficulty, if you can do two things—stop and turn." Eager to test my hypothesis, I impulsively boarded the lift taking me to the top of the mountain's most difficult slope, at which point I formulated another theory: "I'm an idiot." When I got off the lift and skied over to where the run started, I observed what appeared to be an almost vertical drop. Maybe it was just my imagination, but it seemed like everyone around me spoke with European accents and had names like Sven and Bjorn. I considered taking off my skis and walking down, figuring injured pride would be less painful than a broken neck. But as it turned out, my first theory was accurate (and maybe the second one too). I slowly and cautiously zigzagged all the way down, stopping and turning, never losing control. Yes, I fell a few

times, but I never lost control. It took me forever and wore me out, but I survived the descent.

People hate conflict because they hate that out-of-control feeling, which is what happens with bad conflict. But if we do certain things, we can rein conflict in and control it. There are three places of movement inside the bad conflict cycle (see the Appendix), and intervening at any one of these places breaks the cycle and de-escalates tensions. In this chapter we're going to discover more about stopping and turning. We'll discuss how our reason muscles help us escape the gravitational pull of the conflict trap, including how to restrict our buttons, how to respond rather than react, and how to refrain from pushing the other person's buttons.

Restrict Your Buttons

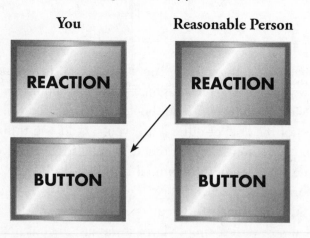

Controlling What Happens to You

When we restrict our buttons, we prevent them from getting pushed so easily. This is expressed through various common phrases:

- Don't let him get to you.
- You need thicker skin.
- You need to guard your heart.

- Don't be so sensitive.
- Don't let him get the best of you.
- Don't take things so personally.
- Don't wear your feelings on your sleeve.
- Don't be goaded; be guarded.

We keep our buttons from getting pushed if we do two things: know our buttons and clarify perceptions.

Know Your Buttons

Locate Them

As discussed in Chapter 2, we all have buttons—or places where we tend to be overly sensitized. We're like minefields where others walk around safely until they step on the mines, resulting in explosions. The explosions—our reactions to button pushing—may be loud or silent and result in fight or flight. Minefields are neutralized by locating the mines and defusing them. And the same is true with our buttons. Answering the following questions may help you locate yours.

- What causes me to react in a way that seems out of proportion to the trigger?
- What really gets on my nerves?
- What are my pet peeves?
- What things do I become easily offended over?
- What causes my blood to boil?
- If my closest friends were answering these questions about me, what would they say?

Understand Them

After mines are located, they must be defused. Unlike mines, we can't actually defuse our buttons, but we can *desensitize* them, which happens when we understand why they are there. Figuring out what caused them won't make them go away, but it does allow us to thicken the skin around them, helps us feel less crazy for having them, and makes them less prone to get pushed. For instance, I had a client once who was constantly criticized by older siblings. As a result, anything in the present that looked, sounded, or smelled like criticism aroused feelings associated with those past experiences. Current criticism, real or imagined, resulted in a reaction that was way out of proportion to the cause (or trigger). He didn't know he had that button, but once he realized it, he was better able to build a shield around it so it wasn't pushed so easily.

C.S. Lewis said, "It's not the remembered past, it's the forgotten past that enslaves us."[1] Understanding our buttons by connecting the dots between the past and present lowers their sensitivity. The same is true for other causes of buttons. Understanding how our brains work, understanding our areas of immaturity, and understanding our particular hot-button convictions will lower the button-pushing likelihood in any of these areas.

Doing a good job of restricting our buttons requires using certain muscles. *Humility* enables us to acknowledge that we have areas of potential weaknesses. *Awareness* enables us to observe them.

When Neil and Laura Clarified Their Buttons

From all appearances, Neil was a smart guy with a healthy IQ. But when it came to articulating his thoughts, he wasn't quick. He could eventually do it, but only with time and effort. Laura, on the other hand, could speak her mind without breaking a sweat. When arguments occurred, Neil's verbal quickness skills had to compete with Laura's, and he lost every contest. When his "articulation" button was pushed, Neil typically reacted by fleeing—shutting down and waiting for the storm to blow past. And that drove Laura crazy.

And then there was Laura's button. She grew up in the home of Ebenezer Scrooge. To say that her dad was a tightwad would be the greatest of understatements. For instance, he once calculated the exact cost of a toilet flush and then lectured the family for what he concluded to be excessive flushes. They weren't poor by anyone's standards but to hear him tell it, they lived one small step away from destitution. Fast-forward a few years into Laura's marriage. Whenever Neil would express fiscal concerns, Laura's "Scrooge" button would get pushed. In reaction, she'd fight by using her well-honed articulation abilities against her verbally challenged opponent. That drove Neil crazy.

Neil's button was caused by the way his brain processed information. Laura's button came about as a result of her past experiences. They both will probably always have those particular areas of sensitivity, but by understanding them and talking openly to each other about them, their buttons became less sensitive. (We'll discuss how to control your reactions when your buttons get pushed later.)

Clarify Your Perceptions

There are two main aspects to understanding our perceptions: correct or confirm our conclusions and consider the context.

Correct the Conclusion

Many conflict problems are ones of *perception*. People jump to conclusions, make mountains out of molehills, misunderstand each other, misread each other, and misinterpret the meaning of words and actions. Concerning this, conflict resolution consultant Dudley Weeks says,

> Perceptions greatly influence the way people and societies mold their attitudes and much of their behavior, and therefore play a major role in the causes of conflict and in the way we deal with it.[2]

Buttons are pushed by misperceptions just as easily as they respond to actual pushes. Misperceptions occur for at least two reasons: misinterpretation and misinformation.

Misinterpretation

During World War II, U.S. President Franklin Roosevelt and

British Prime Minister Winston Churchill held a summit meeting to address a major decision regarding the Allied war effort. The night before their departure, the hour was late, no conclusion had been reached, and tensions were escalating. At one point Churchill stated emphatically, "I think we need to table this matter." Roosevelt vehemently disagreed, arguing that the consequences of not settling the issue could be disastrous. The ensuing argument evaporated when someone in Churchill's entourage clarified the meaning of the prime minister's statement. What Churchill meant was, "We need to put this issue on the table and not give up until it's resolved." At that point, it became clear that the two leaders had been fighting a battle that didn't exist. Roosevelt's button was being pushed by a misinterpretation, assuming that what Churchill meant was, "Let's stop talking and go to bed." His information was accurate—Churchill actually made the statement—but the interpretation was inaccurate. They settled the argument by clarifying the interpretation.

The way to clarify an interpretation is by asking: "What I hear you saying is _____. Am I understanding you correctly?" Clarifying statements such as the following will make the situation worse: "So, what's *that* supposed to mean?" and "What do you mean by *that?*" A positive tone and attitude are crucial to positive clarification. A negative tone and attitude will push the other person's buttons and energize the bad conflict cycle.

Misinformation

I was an undergraduate during the latter days of the Vietnam War era when nightly news was dominated by stories of radical student activism. My southern, relatively conservative university was not exactly the bastion of radicalism, but we had our share of student protests. I'd written a check to a men's store called the "Down Under," so named because it was located under a city street. I'd also written a check to "The Solution Bowl," an after-Christmas conference for college students. I went home one weekend when my dad, who regularly scrutinized my spending practices, inquired,

"What is 'Solution Underground'?" He was concerned I'd joined the Communist Party or been recruited by student militants to blow up ROTC buildings.

As in the Roosevelt and Churchill example, my dad was fighting a battle that didn't exist, not because of misinterpretation, but because of misinformation. His mixed-up information led to a faulty conclusion. I corrected the information by explaining that one check was made out to a men's store and the other was to a conference for Christian college students. Correcting the information cleared the air. He was relieved to learn that his son wasn't a radical.

If our information or knowledge is erroneous or incomplete, the conclusion drawn will be inaccurate. The solution is to correct the information, often referred to as "getting your facts straight." Facts don't speak for themselves; they must be interpreted. And we can't make correct interpretations without accurate information. The best way to do this is to say, "I want to understand this correctly. Will you please clarify for me what actually happened?"

We need all our reason muscles to perform this task. *Humility* enables us to acknowledge that our conclusions could be faulty. *Awareness* and *responsibility* enable us to be bothered when we discover our conclusions are off base. We need our *empathy* muscle to understand the other person, and the *reliability* muscle will enable us to alter our faulty perceptions. The chart below summarizes the differences between the two types of misperceptions.

Categories of Mispercetions

Misperception Resulting from	Type of Information	Type of Conclusion	What to Correct
Misinterpretation	Accurate	Inaccurate	Interpretation
Misinformation	Inaccurate, erroneous, or incomplete	Inaccurate	Information

Consider the Context

My first two children were born during the era when it was trendy to deliver babies without the use of pain-killing drugs. My wife, Penny, and I attended classes to learn about contractions, fetal monitors, breathing exercises, and the information needed to make delivering a baby less mysterious and more predictable. One night the teacher made this prediction: "Dads, toward the end, when the contractions are intense and frequent, your wife may cuss at you and insult your ancestry. Don't be offended, guys. Pain does that to people. It will pass." She was telling us to *consider the context.* Under normal circumstances, such remarks would be highly offensive, but under these special circumstances, there would be no reason to take offense.

If someone is being offensive to us, and we find our buttons being pushed, we need to take the context into consideration. For instance, we should ask ourselves if he or she is...

- in a hurry
- under stress
- distraught
- reacting
- in pain
- medically compromised
- grieving

These are just a few of the many reasons why a person may be offensive even though not intending to be. Taking context factors into consideration enables us to "cut him some slack" or "give her a break," which keeps our buttons from being pushed unnecessarily.

The main muscle needed here is *empathy.* We are placing ourselves into the other person's shoes to understand where he or she is coming from.

When Neil and Laura Clarified Their Perceptions

Neil's experience growing up was just the opposite of Laura's when it came to money issues. In Laura's home, fiscal policy was determined by Ebenezer Scrooge. In Neil's home, there was no fiscal policy, resulting in financial chaos, frivolous spending, mounting debt, unpaid bills, and constant calls from bill collectors. Early on, Neil determined that he would never live under such conditions once he was out of the house. Along with this noble commitment, however, he brought a "money" button with him into adulthood. That is, anything that resembled fiscal irresponsibility elicited an over-the-top reaction.

When they argued over Kevin's Europe trip, Neil's expressions of concern for finances pushed Laura's "Scrooge" button because his statements felt too reminiscent of her father's excessively tight-fisted monetary decrees. In reaction, she'd blurt the attacking remark, "All you care about is money!" He would then react by withdrawing, and the cycle perpetuated.

Laura's conclusion, "All you care about is money," was inaccurate. She had her information right—he *did* express financial concerns—but her interpretation was wrong. Consequently, she was mad at him for a problem that didn't exist. They were having a *perception* problem that came about as a result of *misinterpretation*. And if they didn't clear this up, their efforts to solve the "Kevin going to Europe" problem would constantly be derailed.

I pointed out to Laura that she was making a dogmatic assertion about something that can't be observed directly—Neil's motives. Words and actions are observable; motives and intentions are not. We can state that a person said something, but we can only *speculate* as to what he or she meant when it was said. Only the person who spoke can accurately explain the meaning. By saying authoritatively, "All you care about is money," Laura was presuming to know the real meaning behind Neil's words. People hate being misinterpreted, and Neil reacted in his typical manner—by withdrawing into silence.

To break the cycle, Laura had to *go against her grain* and exercise her empathy muscle. She finally asked this question: "Will you help me understand why this money thing is such a big deal to you?" Neil was then able to explain that he wasn't only concerned about money but feared inadvertently reinforcing Kevin's fiscal irresponsibility. This conversation took a while to work out, but by the end of it Laura had corrected her misinterpretation. Their perception problem was solved, thus ending this particular battle.

This wasn't their only perception problem, and each was guilty of misperceiving the other from time to time. But they learned to clarify their perceptions whenever necessary, thereby breaking their cycle of bad conflict.

Respond Rather Than React

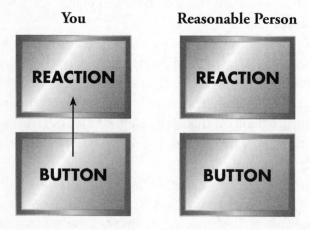

Controlling What You Display

You | Reasonable Person

REACTION | REACTION

BUTTON | BUTTON

The second place to break the bad conflict cycle is at the level of our reactions. The idea is to turn automatic, knee-jerk reactions into chosen *responses*. Remember, reactions fall into two categories—fight or flight. Reactions, whatever the form, tend to push the other person's buttons, perpetuating the negative cycle. We can do two things to break the cycle: preplan our responses and stop to think.

Preplan Your Responses

Having grown up in the Deep South, I never had much occasion to drive on ice. After graduating from college, I took a job up North where snow and icy conditions were commonplace for several months of the year. The first time I hit an icy patch, I reacted by turning the wheel in who knows what direction, resulting in my car doing a complete 360. I lived to tell the tale. After recounting the event, I was told by one of my northern friends that when a car hits ice, the driver should keep his foot off the brake and keep the front wheels turned in the direction of the slide. I mentally rehearsed this scenario many times, and when it happened again, I did what I'd rehearsed. It worked. I had replaced my knee-jerk reaction with a preplanned response.

Rehearsing our responses, anticipating button pushes, and knowing how we will respond ahead of time alters our behavior. Otherwise, in the heat of the moment, our choices will be governed by natural impulses, and the situation probably won't go well. Pilots, firefighters, police, paramedics, and soldiers are trained to function under pressure. Their responses to certain situations are taught ahead of time, and they repeatedly practice those responses in simulations until they become second nature. Athletes refer to this as "muscle memory." They practice something enough times that when the situation calls for it, their muscle memory kicks in, and they can perform the actions without having to think about each step. People in conflict are under pressure, and preplanned responses keep them steady.

If our natural tendency is to blow up (fight) when certain buttons get pushed, we need a rehearsable repertoire of responses that will enable us to avoid the explosions. For example, we can…

- politely excuse ourselves and leave the premises
- bite our tongues and say nothing
- say, "I don't want to blow up at you. So let me collect my thoughts before I respond. Otherwise, I'm afraid it will come out badly."

If we are naturally prone to withdraw (flight) in reaction to button pushes, our repertoire of choices might include:

- ask questions to keep us engaged in the conversation
- explain what's going on inside our heads at the moment. This is an *announced withdrawal*: "I feel my turtle tendencies kicking in right now. I'm not trying to shut you out, but I need a few minutes to respond. Bear with me."

The best alternative to a fight reaction is honest, civil conversation. The best alternative to a flight reaction is also honest civil conversation. Tigers need to be more civil, while turtles need to converse more. We can be tigers, turtles, or talkers. Preplanned responses increase the likelihood of honest, civil conversations, which are less likely to push buttons.

When Neil and Laura Preplanned Their Responses

Laura was most often a fight reactor—a tiger. Neil, on the other hand, was a flight reactor—a turtle. He would go into his shell in reaction to her tiger roar, which, in turn, elicited louder roars. Before they came to counseling, they understood this pattern and how stuck they were in it. What they failed to understand was its destructiveness and how to change it. And this pattern would never change without them countering their natural reactive tendencies.

Laura came to realize that when she reacted with open displays of shrillness and anger, Neil would run for cover and nothing would be accomplished. Yes, she was still angry, but she *chose* not to display it in ways that had a button-pushing effect on Neil. Instead of reacting through statements like "Well, it wouldn't hurt you to darken the door of God's house every now and then either, Mr. Pagan," she planned and rehearsed civil statements such as, "Church is important to me, and I'd love it if we could go together. I'd like us to discuss that sometime, if not now then later." This was neither easy nor familiar, and it felt peculiar to her the first several times she did it. It was like writing with her nondominant hand.

Neil realized that his open displays of withdrawal didn't help either. Instead of shutting down and shutting up, he developed some statements to use when he was inclined to retreat. Instead of saying, "It just doesn't do any good to talk about it," he started saying, "You know me. When we argue, I tend to shut down and stop talking. I'm not shutting down right now, I'm just thinking. Give me a minute so I can figure out the best way to say what's on my mind." This felt just as odd to Neil as Laura's chosen responses felt to her, but they eventually got past the strangeness and appreciated the improved communication.

Stop and Think

What if we get caught off guard, finding ourselves reacting with no previously rehearsed alternative response? What do we do then? Here's a refresher lesson from Psych 101. A stimulus elicits an automatic reaction. If we want to turn the automatic reaction into a chosen response, we must insert an intervening variable between the two. That intervening variable is called *thought*. People in conflict are very prone to either attack first and think later or to withdraw first and think later. The order needs to be reversed. If we hit pause on our action and press the think button, we can choose what our response will be *before resuming* the action. It's not easy, but it's doable if we're aware of the need for it and set about to deliberately make it happen.

When Neil and Laura Stopped and Thought

Neil and Laura were bright, articulate people, though Neil expressed himself more slowly. Reactions to button pushes were lightning-quick on both sides. Sometimes their well-intentioned, preplanned responses were lost in the haze and confusion of battle. Before they knew it, Laura would launch her artillery barrage, and Neil would climb into his bunker to wait for the shelling to cease.

I made a suggestion to Laura. I proposed that she go to a car dealership and have them install a clutch between her brain and her mouth. That way she could push in the clutch and think before spewing the angry words coursing through her brain. I also made a suggestion to Neil. I proposed that he have the same dealership install a cable connecting his brain and his mouth. That way he could utter some of the words he was thinking rather than remaining silent. Fortunately, they both laughed and got the point.

"Reason muscles" require us to go against the grain of our natural inclinations. *Awareness* enables us to see the destructiveness of reacting, *responsibility* enables us to cringe when it happens, and *reliability* gives us the strength to change those reactions into responses.

Refrain from Pushing Buttons

Controlling What You Do to Others

The third way to break the cycle of bad conflict is to refrain from pushing buttons. Pushing buttons is expressed through phrases such as:

- He attacks the person instead of the problem.
- His campaign has taken the low road.
- That was a low blow.

- He's really taken the gloves off.
- She's adding fuel to the fire.
- I let him have it with both barrels.
- They fight dirty.
- She really steps on toes.
- She hits below the belt.
- Their arguments have become nasty and personal.

Pushing the other person's buttons triggers automatic defensive reactions, and the bad conflict cycle continues. In order to refrain from pushing buttons, we must heed the other person's buttons and restrain our attacks.

Heed the Other's Buttons

Good conflict requires that we know our own buttons and those of the other person we're involved with. If we live with or work with that person in close quarters, the probability of button pushing is high. Sometimes a button is pushed inadvertently or out of ignorance because the button pusher is unaware of or forgot about its existence. To keep that from happening, we must know the location of the other person's "land mines" and be careful not to step there. All of the mine location questions we ask about ourselves should also be asked about the other person:

- What causes him or her to react in a way that seems out of proportion to the trigger?
- What really gets on his or her nerves?
- What are his or her pet peeves?
- About what things does he or she become easily offended?
- What causes his or her blood to boil?
- If his or her closest friends were answering these questions, what would they say?

When Neil and Laura Heeded Each Other's Buttons

At least some of the arguments between Neil and Laura started because one of them would say or do something out of ignorance, and it had a button-pushing effect. For instance, during one session, we were within striking distance of resolving their difference of opinion about Kevin's Europe trip using the process we'll discuss in Chapter 5. The negotiated solution was hard fought and the peace agreement was still uncertain when, at the most precisely inopportune time, Neil turned to Laura and blurted, "I'm OK with him going as long as the two of you don't go out and brainlessly spend us into oblivion."

From everything I could tell, Neil had just experienced an attack of "sudden onset stupidity." Why, when things were so delicate, would he use words that would obviously pummel Laura's "Scrooge" button with a steel bat? Predictably, Laura reacted by screeching, "See, you don't give a flip about your son! All you care about is the almighty dollar!" This, of course, reignited the bad conflict cycle war. Unfortunately, we lost valuable ground that had to be regained.

I don't think Neil did this on purpose. He would have done well to pay attention to this pre-blurt thought:

> If I say what I'm about to say, it will probably push that button of hers that makes her so sensitive about finances. And when that button gets pushed, watch out! I better not say that.

On the other hand, it probably wouldn't have pushed any buttons had Neil said:

> I feel good about this agreement because it satisfies your concern about cultural enrichment and my concern about fiscal responsibility. If we stick to this, I think it'll work.

Restrain Your Attacks

While buttons may be pushed inadvertently, they are sometimes pushed on purpose to attack, to score points. A person will sometimes unburden himself (or herself) by "getting it off his chest" or letting the other person "have it." This hammering technique is often justified under the banner of "being bold," "being honest," or "just saying what I feel." Actually, it's not being bold, it's being vindictive. Exacting revenge is the more probable motivation. Professor Howard Hendricks, Dallas Theological Seminary, tells of a woman in conflict who boasted that she gave the other person a piece of her mind. Hendricks remarked, "Unfortunately, it was a piece of her mind she really couldn't afford to lose."

Revenge also motivates some people to punish the other person with isolation and silence. In such cases, this is the internal dialogue: "I'll just freeze her out and not talk to her for a while. We'll just see how she likes that. That'll teach her."

The problem with attacks of any kind is that the other person rarely learns what we're trying to teach. They often miss the point if we're intent on scoring points. He or she is too busy retaliating, and this energizes the bad conflict cycle. So what we need are alternatives to attacking.

Punch Pause

Sometimes conditions exist that have to be rectified prior to a surgical procedure. Performing the surgery without first clearing up the condition may jeopardize the patient's life. There are times when continuing to discuss a conflict problem is unwise because conditions exist that undercut the likelihood of success. Such conditions may include fatigue, multiple pressures, limited time, limited privacy, and illness. For instance, a couple may agree, "We're both so tired that we shouldn't keep discussing this tonight. Let's pick it back up in the morning after we've had some rest." A pause in the action gives us a chance to improve the conditions so that when the action is resumed, we're more likely to succeed.

Pick Your Battles

When we argue we tend to discuss multiple topics simultaneously. (We'll look more at this in Chapter 5.) Sometimes it's best to focus on certain issues and let the others go for the time being. On occasion we may even decide to lay an issue down and not bring it back up for discussion, at least for now. This may be the case if the time and place are not conducive, bringing it up is certain to trigger defensiveness, or we perceive that the other person won't get it no matter how well we say it. It's important to distinguish this action from conflict avoidance, in which we think, *I hate arguing, so I'm not going to bring it up.* There's a difference between being avoidant and being wise. Picking our battles means, "In the scheme of things, this is not that big of a deal. I want us to spend our energies solving more important problems, so I'm choosing to let this one go."

Perform Acts of Kindness

Instead of attacking the person, we deliberately do something nice. For instance, in the heat of battle a husband walks over to his wife, gives her a hug, and says, "I hate when we get stuck like this. We'll figure this out. I love you." When his wife gets up off the floor, she'll probably feel less defensive and reactive. This is often referred to as "being the bigger person." It's difficult to pull this off because it requires us to counter that internal voice that says, *This isn't fair. Why do I have to be the bigger person?* The reason is that it helps the system and, if the system improves, both parties are ultimately helped. Being kind instead of attacking breaks the cycle of bad conflict, which is worth doing because as long as the cycle continues, no problems get solved.

Pay Attention to Your Delivery

Preface your remarks. Before a dentist sticks us with that long hypodermic to deaden the nerves around a tooth, he'll usually say, "OK, you're going to feel a little sting." The warning enables us to brace ourselves so we won't react by jumping out of the chair. In the same way, prefacing our remarks braces the other person and lowers the likelihood of reaction. Here are some examples.

- I don't mean this the way it might sound, but…
- Please don't take this personally…
- This might sound offensive, but I need you to hear me out on this…

Watch your tone and body language. We've all heard that communication takes place through the words we use, how we sound when we're saying them (tone), and how we look when we're saying them (body language). Studies show that the percentage of communication attributable to words is usually around 10 to 15 percent. The remaining 85 to 90 percent is attributable to tone and body language. Consequently, if a discrepancy exists between the words used and one of the other factors, more weight is given to the other factors. That's why people say, "How you say it is so loud that I can't actually hear what you say." The people feel attacked not by what's said but by the delivery.

For instance, suppose you're trying to restrain your attacks by hitting pause. You say, "We're both so tired that we shouldn't keep discussing this tonight. Let's pick it back up in the morning after we have had some rest." You use exactly the right words, but you deliver them using a whispery, sarcastic, singsong quality and place air quotations with your fingers around the word "we." The other person, not surprisingly, feels attacked because of the discrepancy between your words, tone, and body language. He or she doesn't hear the message of the words but hears, "I'm fine. *You're* the problem. Maybe if *you* get some rest, *you'll* be less crazy." That conceptual threat pushes a button that leads to an inevitable reaction—and the negative cycle continues.

I've suggested to couples on occasion that they communicate through writing letters, on the phone, through email, or while not looking at each other. Sometimes the message of the words comes across more effectively by removing tone or body language factors from the mix.

Use "I" language instead of "you" language. We get mad when we argue. That's understandable. Being angry is not the problem, displaying it in the wrong way is. We can be angry at someone and express it in ways that have less of a button-pushing effect. One way to do this is through the use of "I" language, which is less likely to leave the other person feeling personally attacked. Notice which of these examples are more likely to push buttons.

> *You:* You made me mad tonight when you told that "cute" little joke about me.
>
> *I:*   I need to tell you about something that bothered me tonight. I'm angry about the joke you told at my expense. I didn't like it when you did that.

> *You:* You're late, as usual.
>
> *I:*   It inconveniences me when you arrive late.

> *You:* You just interrupted again!
>
> *I:*   It bothers me when you interrupt.

Notice that what distinguishes one from the other is not the use of the words "I" or "you" so much as where the emphasis is placed. If the focus is on the other person, he or she feels attacked and is more likely to react. Keeping the focus on our side lowers that likelihood.

Don't use superlatives. Terms such as *always* or *never* push buttons because the other person feels like his or her character is being attacked more than the behavior. To have less of a button-pushing effect, it's better to use phrases such as:

- as a general rule
- it seems to be a pattern
- often
- sometimes
- rarely

When Neil and Laura Restrained Their Attacks

From the outset, I had a ringside view of Neil and Laura's verbal fistfights. Zingers like "Mr. Pagan" were counterpunched with statements like "That self-righteous tone of hers reminds me so much of her mother, I could just throw up." My front-row seat was constantly being splattered with blood, sweat, and tears.

In a candid moment, Laura admitted that she sometimes attacked Neil on purpose, deliberately pushing his buttons to get a rise out of him. In her opinion, they never resolved anything because Neil ran away from conflict. So new arguments became opportunities to resurrect old, unsolved problems—which she did viciously. Her internal dialogue said, *What have I got to lose? He won't ever talk to me so I might as well use this occasion to bring up everything I can think of.* She eventually came to realize that all of these attacks never accomplished anything. Neil would either counterpunch or crawl further into his shell, never getting the point she was trying to make. And Neil admitted that he sometimes withdrew on purpose, hoping she would feel punished and get the point he was trying to make—"Stop yelling!" But that never worked either.

Laura had been operating under the assumption that saying it louder would make it heard. Actually, the louder she said it, the more Neil pressed the mute button inside his head so he didn't have to hear it. Neil was under the mistaken assumption that pressing mute would make Laura and the problem go away. But the more he withdrew, the shriller Laura became. He wasn't using words, but the message communicated by his silence was highly offensive. He felt attacked by her words, and she felt attacked by his silence.

Laura had a delivery problem. Realizing its impact, she worked hard to ratchet down her shrillness. She made use of what's taught in this adage: "You catch more flies with molasses than with vinegar." By saying it differently, Neil started hearing what she said. Neil also had a delivery problem—no delivery at all. But the impact of no delivery sent a loud message nonetheless. With that realization, he started talking more, taking his thoughts and putting them into words. As a result, Laura was able to better understand his viewpoint. Restraining their attacks didn't solve all of their problems right away, but it created some ground on which they could stand to solve them later.

As with all other aspects of good conflict, restraining their attack impulses went against every natural inclination. The main muscle needed here was *empathy,* which enabled each one to consider the impact of his or her words and actions on the other. The impulse was to inflict hurt, and stronger empathy muscles enabled both of them to restrain that impulse.

Good conflict requires "reason muscles" (see Chapter 3) to exit and stay out of the conflict trap (Chapter 4). Doing so enables us to solve the problems causing the conflict (Chapter 5). The following table below summarizes what's needed to flee the trap of bad conflict.

Fleeing the Bad Conflict Trap

Action to Take	Methods to Use	Muscles Needed
RESTRICT your buttons	Know your buttons Clarify your perceptions	Humility Awareness
RESPOND rather than react	Preplan your responses Stop and think	Awareness Responsibility Reliability
REFRAIN from pushing buttons	Heed the other's buttons Restrain your attacks	Empathy

In a Nutshell

We exit the conflict trap by stopping the cycle of bad conflict at any one of three places. First, we control what happens to us by *restricting our buttons,* keeping them from being so easily pushed. Second, we control what we display by turning our natural reactions into *chosen responses.* Third, we control what we do to others by *refraining from pushing their buttons,* thus stopping the negative cycle.

For Reflection

1. How do your perceptions influence your reactions?

2. Which "reason muscles" help you avoid reacting to button pushing?

3. What does context have to do with perceptions and protecting your buttons?

4. Describe the difference between *responding* and *reacting.*

5. What is the best alternative to a fight reaction? A flight reaction? Can you give a personal example of each?

6. When do you push someone's buttons deliberately? What results?

7. What is the difference between picking your battles and conflict avoidance?

Chapter 5

FIXING THE PROBLEMS

*I have a horror of words that are not translated
into actions, of speech that does not result in deeds.*
TEDDY ROOSEVELT

*Overlook an offense and bond a friendship;
fasten on to a slight and—good-bye, friend!*
PROVERBS 17:9

I teach this stuff at work," a client of mine said after hearing me explain what's involved in fixing a conflict problem. "But I don't do it at home," he sheepishly admitted. Another client, an attorney, told me, "You know, I practice litigation and argue for a living. When I'm in court, the Rules of Civil Procedure ensure that there is order to the process. But when I come home and argue with my wife, there are no rules. I hate that."

What we'll go over in this chapter is often applied more readily to business and professional settings than it is to personal relationships. A judge or a parliamentarian may require adherence to the process in formal settings, but nobody makes us do this at home or with our friends.

We'll look at five questions that need to be answered for a conflict problem to be solved. Doing conflict the good way requires answering all of them. Missing one will put us right back into the bad conflict trap—the conflict conversation will shut down and the problem causing the conflict will remain unsolved. If we're not used to doing this process, it may feel cumbersome and tedious for a while. But, like

111

learning to drive a car or use a computer, it becomes second nature once we gain knowledge of it and do it routinely.

Question 1: Which problem are we trying to fix?

On occasion I attend meetings run by parliamentary procedure. The following statements are frequently heard in those gatherings:

- I'd like to make a motion that _____.
- Is there a second?
- We're now open for discussion on the motion.
- Your remarks are out of order.
- Any further discussion?
- All in favor say aye. Those opposed, by like sign.
- The ayes have it.
- The motion failed.

I usually hate those meetings because the deliberations feel stilted and cumbersome. And yet motions are made and discussed one at a time, votes are taken, and problems are solved. If we didn't go about it that way, the meetings would degenerate into free-for-all discussions of multiple issues that would end without one problem being solved. Mediators, those trained in the techniques of Alternative Dispute Resolution, experience a very high rate of success.[1] Why? Because they purposely isolate the specific problem needing resolution and then follow clearly defined procedures to solve it. Negotiators follow a similar procedure.[2]

Unfortunately, when people argue outside a business setting, disputes are seldom governed by anything like Robert's Rules of Order, the Rules of Civil Procedure, Alternative Dispute Resolution principles, or negotiation techniques. Consequently, they are prone to argue in an unstructured way about multiple problems simultaneously. And when the conversation is over, the problem that started the argument usually remains unsolved.

When *Saving Private Ryan* was released, survivors of the Normandy invasion were asked to give their opinions of the film. Many of them said something to the effect of, "More than any film I've ever seen, this movie captures the utter confusion of battle." Battle is confusing regardless of the setting—between soldiers in combat, between spouses, between co-workers, between church members, between neighbors, between parents and children. Conflict becomes less confusing if we learn to do personally what mediators, negotiators, and parliamentarians do professionally. That is, we must identify individual problems and then solve them one at a time.

Understand the Types of Problems

Pay attention the next time you're in an argument or hear an argument. You'll probably notice at least four types of conflict problems:

- *Preference problems.* These problems result from actual differences. One person prefers to do it one way, and the other person prefers to do it another way. The differences of opinion may be significant or trivial.

- *Perception problems.* These problems result from perceived differences. One person inaccurately attributes meaning to the words or actions of the other person.

- *Process problems.* These problems result from falling into the trap of bad conflict, such as buttons getting pushed, reactions taking over, and pushing the other's buttons. For instance, in the middle of a conflict conversation, one person pushes the other person's buttons by being sarcastic. Suddenly the argument now involves two topics—the original issue plus a new one, the person's sarcasm.

- *Pressure problems.* These are circumstances that make solving conflict problems more difficult. Pressures from outside the relationship drain the time and energy needed to solve problems inside the relationship. For instance, some couples are so pressured by limited time that they never sit down and work things through. Other examples of pressure problems include financial difficulties, health problems, fatigue, and lack of privacy.

We solve *perception* problems by clearing up misperceptions. We solve *process* problems by restricting our buttons, responding rather than reacting, and refraining from pushing buttons. We solve *pressure* problems by acknowledging their effects and making the necessary adjustments. *Preference* problems are solved by answering all five of the questions described in this chapter.

Fix One Problem at a Time

Here's what happens in many arguments. The conflict starts over a problem of perception or preference. During the discussion, one person commits a process error, which triggers the other person's process error. Tensions escalate and, in that state of heightened sensitivities, additional perception problems occur, such as, "What's that look supposed to mean?" This leads to additional process errors. "As long as we're at it" attitudes prevail, and previously unsolved perception or preference problems get brought up and added to the mix. Before we know it, the number of problems being simultaneously discussed is in the double digits. Finally someone says, "I don't have time to talk about this right now"—a pressure problem. The argument is so frustrating and unproductive that neither one wants to bring it up later. Consequently, whatever started the argument in the first place gets added to the list of unsolved problems.

It was this frustration that brought Neil and Laura to my office. In the introduction to this section, I gave a synopsis of my first session with them. If we were to analyze their dialogue and count the number of problems, here's what we'd find:

2   pressure problems

10   process problems

5   perception problems

7   preference problems
_____

24   problems

This one argument, which probably lasted 1 to 2 minutes, contained 24 separate problems, each of which screamed for resolution. Neil and Laura couldn't solve any individual problem because they argued about all of them simultaneously. Like a jumbled mass of electrical wires with the insulation rubbed off, each problem carried an emotional charge, which triggered all the others. And the longer they talked, the more problems were added to the list.

How can we solve 24 problems at the same time? We can't! And to attempt it is to set ourselves up to fail. So we must have a clear answer to our first conflict resolution question: "Which problem are we trying to fix?" When couples argue in my office, I will sometimes call a time-out and ask them to answer this question. Most often, they give me two different answers...and I usually have a third one. To solve problems, we must focus on them one at a time.

Answering the next four questions requires an unambiguous answer to the first question. Sounds easy enough, right? Even if this question is answered clearly, we still get sidetracked when other problems pop up during an argument. When this happens, we have two options.

Hit Pause, Fix the Problem, Hit Resume

This means that we stop the discussion of the selected problem, quickly address the new one, and get back to the previous discussion. For instance, suppose you've narrowed your focus to one issue but, while discussing it, a process problem pops up. Your opponent says, "Well, excuse me, Mr. Smarter-Than-Anyone-Else." Your natural inclination would be to react by saying, "Well, I'm certainly smarter than you, idiot." If that happened, the focus on the original problem would be lost while the two of you veer off into IQ comparisons. Instead, handle it this way:

> Look, we're going to accomplish a whole lot more if we can drop the use of sarcasm. I'm trying to avoid sarcasm with you and would appreciate it if you wouldn't be sarcastic with me. Can we agree on that?

If your opponent agrees, you can get back to discussing the first issue. Also, if a new subject gets introduced into the current discussion, it helps to say, "That's an important topic, but it's not the one we're discussing right now. Let's make note of it and come back to it later. Okay?"

Ignore It and Stay on Track

Sometimes it helps to just ignore the new problem. Let's take the same example in which you're called "Mr. Smarter-Than-Anyone Else." Your internal dialogue might sound like this:

> *Boy, that was really snotty. Everything in me wants to fire back right now, and I could. Oh, could I ever! But if I did, the discussion would get sidetracked, and we really need to get this thing resolved. So I'm going to ignore the comment. I'm not going there. I'm going to keep my cool and stay on subject.*

At a later time you may choose to give this problem—the use of sarcasm in arguments—its own focus.

When Neil and Laura Selected One Problem to Fix

What made Neil and Laura's verbal battle so confusing, even to me, was they weren't arguing about 1 thing but 24 things. Their skirmishes bounced from one emotionally charged issue to another. When the conversation ended, nothing was resolved. I felt like I was listening to 24 different radio stations at the same time. If they couldn't focus on and fix even 1 problem, they'd likely go home thinking, *Well, that was a waste of time.* And they'd be right. Trying to fix everything simultaneously would result in nothing being fixed.

At one point I called a time-out and asked them to select just one problem to focus on. After sparring for a few rounds, they selected the issue of Kevin's Europe trip, a *preference* problem about which they had different opinions: Laura wanted Kevin to go; Neil did not.

Even after they selected a focus, other problems kept popping up during the deliberations. Laura would say, "All you care about is money," a *perception* problem. Neil's flight reaction would kick in, leading him to fall silent, a *process* problem. Or something in the discussion would remind one of them of some other unsolved *preference* problem. Attention was diverted by these side issues repeatedly so the main issue of Kevin's trip was lost. This commonly occurs in arguments. To solve this particular difference of opinion, Neil and Laura would have to deliberately address the issues. Sometimes they would stop the action, talk about the other problem, and then get back to the main issue. For instance, when Neil would fall silent, Laura would say, "This discussion will go much better if, instead of being silent, you tell me what you're thinking. Will you do that for me, please?" At other times, they simply ignored the other problem to serve the larger purpose—staying on track.

We need all our reason muscles to answer this question: Which problem are we trying to fix? The awareness muscle is especially important. It enables us to step back and focus on one particular problem.

Now we're ready for the second question.

Question 2: Why do we feel so strongly?

Once the problem is selected, the most natural tendency is to argue vigorously for our particular way to fix it. Energy is then devoted to getting our point across rather than understanding the other person's viewpoint. Discussions change into sparring matches over whose preferences have greater validity, neither side feels understood by the other, and tensions escalate.

Instead of convincing the other person that our view is right, we need to focus on understanding the other person's view. Why does he or she feel so strongly that it must be done that particular way? A mutual commitment to answer this question de-escalates the conflict tension and provides a springboard for answering the other questions.

Answering this second question enables both people to feel *validated*. Remember, validation doesn't mean you agree with the other person but that you understand him or her. Validation occurs when the other person is convinced you get it. Agreement would be nice, but validation is essential because the higher the validation, the lower the conflict tension. The goal of answering this second question is mutual validation, which occurs when both people can complete the following sentences:

- He sees things the ways he does because...
- The reasons she wants to do it that way are...
- This is such a big deal to him because...
- She feels so strongly about this because...

When Neil and Laura Validated Each Other's Preferences

Neil and Laura were making a common mistake. Each ascribed to the other inaccurate motives for the chosen preference. For example, Laura stated emphatically that Neil's only concern was financial—"All you care about is money." That's why he was against the trip. Neil sarcastically exclaimed that Laura had "spoiled the kids rotten." That's why she was for the trip. Erroneous conclusions were drawn because neither questioned and listened to the other. To establish accuracy, they had to willingly suspend their previously drawn conclusions and give the other person a chance to correct them. That wasn't easy or natural.

Finally they asked questions, listened to the answers, and sought to understand what was being heard. When Laura probed a little deeper into Neil's financial sensitivities, she found that her simplistic conclusions were inaccurate. It wasn't that Neil only cared about money but that Kevin seemingly had no concern about finances. Neil feared that simply giving him the trip would deprive him of an opportunity to learn some important financial lessons. When Neil better understood Laura's position, he realized that he had been wrong as well. It wasn't that Laura was spoiling Kevin. She wanted to provide him with enriching experiences, the kind she was never allowed to have.

Through taking time to study the reasons for each other's preferences, they came to understand that they shared a common goal—Kevin's best interest. Where they differed was on how to get there. Once they understood that each of them had a valid rationale for the chosen preference, they quit arguing about whose reasons had the greater validity.

The main muscle needed to answer the second question, "Why do we feel so strongly?" is *empathy,* which enables us to see things from the other person's perspective.

Question 3: How can we agree to fix this?

By asking the second question, we are trying to understand the interests reflected in the preference chosen. By asking this third question, we want to find a solution that most closely satisfies the interests of both sides. We're looking for a solution that can be supported by both people. Often, clarifying the reasons behind each other's chosen preferences makes finding a solution less difficult. Psychologist Susan Heitler says,

> Solution-building is often surprisingly easy. After two initially antagonistic parties have cooperatively explored their underlying concerns, they most often discover that their apparent conflict involved concerns that are complementary. One creative solution can make everyone happy.[3]

In order of desirability, I offer five options for discovering a solution. While the first option is certainly the most preferred, any of them are legitimate ways to resolve a difference. In fact, good conflict relationships will experience all five of these solutions over the course of time.

Our Way

Sometimes referred to as *collaboration*[4] or a *win–win* solution, this option equally satisfies the interests of both sides. The difference is resolved in a way that enables both sides to get what they want.

Partly Both Ways

This is often referred to as *compromise*. Each side gives up something to achieve a solution. It may not be our first preference, but we can live with it.

Your Way

This is referred to as *deferring* and occurs when one party willingly lays aside his or her preference and goes along with the wishes of the other. There are healthy and unhealthy ways of deferring.

Healthy Deferring

In order to serve a larger relational purpose, the one deferring does so willingly and without resentment. His or her stance is, "Even though I have a different preference, I'm willing to do this your way and be OK with it." Sometimes a person will say, "That's not a hill I'm willing to die on." In other words, he or she can give up his preference and be satisfied with it. When deferring is done healthily, no one keeps score because the problem is solved and forgotten.

Unhealthy Deferring

When a person defers to the other grudgingly, as a way to end the argument, the result is lingering resentment. The internal or external dialogue may include:

- All right, all right! If it will get you off my back, you can have it your way. Satisfied?
- Fine! We'll do it your way.
- Whatever you say, dear.
- Whatever.

Deferring may sometimes be done out of fear, anticipating undesirable consequences for disagreement. Unhealthy deferring can't be done without scorekeeping, the thought being, *You win this time. But next time, it's my turn. You owe me.*

Wait

Sometimes we get stuck, and no mutual solution seems attainable. At those times, it may be necessary to back off, take a break, and lay the problem down for a while. This is an agreed upon truce, a cease-fire, a discussion moratorium that allows tensions to de-escalate and gives both sides time to consider other solution options. There are healthy and unhealthy forms of waiting.

Healthy Waiting

We decide to "sleep on it" before resuming discussion. Oftentimes what appears to be such a big deal today seems insignificant tomorrow. Allowing for extra time may enable both sides to consider a different perspective. A healthy cease-fire arrangement goes like this: "We can't figure out how to resolve this just yet, so we're going to drop the discussion for the time being, but we'll continue it later." The purpose of waiting is to increase our chances of resolution.

Unhealthy Waiting

When the discussion is dropped and not picked up later, that's unhealthy. The problem remains unsolved. This form of waiting is simply a flight reaction. For this reason, a spouse will say, "Sure, he (or she) would like to drop the subject because he (or she) doesn't want to

talk about it. Conveniently, he (or she) will never bring it up again."
The purpose of unhealthy waiting is to avoid conflict, and when conflict is avoided forever no problems are solved.

No Way

Often referred to as an *impasse,* this occurs when no mutually
agreeable solution can be found. The sides are unable to "see eye to
eye" or have a "meeting of the minds." Again, there are healthy and
unhealthy forms of impasse.

Healthy Impasse

This is sometimes called "agreeing to disagree agreeably." The differences are understood and accepted, but they are not allowed to derail
the relationship. The value of the relationship is considered higher
than the need to agree on everything. A healthy impasse focuses less
on what divides and more on what unites. We draw big circles around
the land mines and agree not to step inside those circles. We agree to
be friendly despite our differences. Couples who do this can say, "We
may always disagree on this, but we love each other anyway." This
explains how people with significant incompatibilities are able to relate
to each other so well. We're all familiar with couples—some famous,
some not—who have good marriages despite polar opposite political
philosophies. They are at an impasse politically but have good marriages nonetheless.

Unhealthy Impasse

When both sides disagree and fail to define their impasse in open
terms, it's unhealthy. Since they avoid ever discussing the disagreement,
the problem has tremendous power. No circles are drawn around the
land mines, so the people don't feel safe to be close. The result is a
relationship characterized by alienation and mistrust. More focus is
given to what divides than to what unites. The unspoken arrangement
is, *We have this issue between us that we can't ever talk about, so we better
avoid it at all costs.* Consequently, there are "elephants in the living

room" that are never acknowledged or never discussed. They continue to occupy huge amounts of relational space. While the "our way" solution is *win–win,* this solution is *lose–lose.* No one gains anything by settling differences in this manner.

When Neil and Laura Settled on a Mutual Solution

Neil and Laura had sparred about Kevin's trip but never came to a conclusion. They discussed it simultaneously with zillions of other unsolved problems. Now they singled it out for discussion and took some time to understand the reasons behind their differing preferences.

They had rarely gotten as far as this third question, "How can we agree to fix this?" so this was new territory. They were attempting to resolve their difference in a way that met both sets of interests. Actually, once they set their sights on this goal, it wasn't as hard as they thought. They decided to let Kevin take the Europe trip the next year instead of this year. This satisfied Laura's desire for Kevin to have a culturally enriching experience. In the meantime, Kevin would get a job and earn the money to pay for part of the trip, satisfying Neil's concern about Kevin's sense of entitlement. This gave them a *collaborative, win–win, our way* solution that satisfied Laura's interests as well as Neil's.

This solution wasn't particularly brilliant. It had been there all along, but they hadn't been looking for it because they never stopped and asked, "How can we agree to fix this?" Instead they had been privately asking themselves another question: "What can I do to get him/her to see my side?" Once they started asking the right questions, the answer became apparent. I'm not suggesting this process was quick and painless. They both struggled with it, and it took some time. But like everything else about good conflict, it was doable despite the difficulty.

This couple later asked themselves the same questions about other selected problems, including church attendance. Laura wanted the family to go, but Neil had no interest in attending. No matter how much they talked about it, they never saw eye to eye. They were at an *impasse* but decided to handle it the healthy way. They agreed that Laura would attend church, and Neil would stay home. They would drop it as a subject since arguing about it got them nowhere. They would focus, instead, on the agreeable parts of their relationship.

Another sore spot was the amount and quality of time they spent together. Laura wanted more interaction with Neil when he got home. Neil wanted to turn off his brain when he got home, which meant he was more attracted to mind-numbing television than he was to enthralling conversation. Instead of continuing to spar over this issue, they found a way to *compromise.* Two nights a week, they would leave the house and go somewhere together. It might be to the mall, to a fast-food restaurant, or to a coffee shop—anyplace where they could have some undistracted talk time. On the other nights, Neil could sit in his chair and vegetate, losing himself in the world of sports, talking heads, and reality TV. This mutual solution gave Laura some of what she wanted and Neil some of what he wanted. Even though it was less than each preferred, it was worth it because the problem was solved—and that felt great!

The *humility* muscle is needed to answer this third question. This muscle enables us to allow for opinions that differ from ours as we search for mutual solutions.

Question 4: What will we do to implement it?

Many people attend financial seminars in which they are taught to fix money problems. The reason those systems work is because participants are required to form a structure. They not only establish financial objectives, but they lay down tracks that will take them from here to there. Answering the fourth question enables us to form a structure—to define our options in specific terms so that actions follow statements of intent. We need clear-cut ways to measure whether or not the option is implemented. Otherwise it won't happen, and we'll end up fighting the same battle again and again. Declaration without implementation leads to problem continuation. We must be able to answer this question: "Specifically, what will we do to ensure that our solution comes to pass?"

When Neil and Laura Formed a Structure

Neil and Laura were mutually satisfied with their decision regarding Kevin's Europe trip. But they also knew that if they didn't lay out a specific game plan for Kevin to follow, they'd be right back in the same boat next summer. So here's what they did.

- They sat down with Kevin and determined how much money he would need for the trip.

- They verified this figure with the school.

- They calculated how much he would need to save per month, and how much work would generate that income.

- They went to the bank and set up a personal savings account so he could deposit his income.

- They established deadlines for finding employment and gave him suggestions for places to interview.

- They made sure Kevin knew the deadline for turning in the money and told him unambiguously that if he didn't have it by that point, he wouldn't be going.

Not surprisingly, Kevin grumbled a few remarks under his breath about the "trip Nazis." He was right in a sense. His parents had set up a benevolent dictatorship that cultivated his growth while giving him responsible ways to experience pleasurable opportunities.

The main muscle needed was *reliability,* which ensured that their statements of intent were followed by actions that reflected their intentions.

Question 5: When will we evaluate it?

Imagine a car dealership with this sign out front: "New cars, fully-loaded, half-price. Get 'em while they last!" A guy with bad hair and a bad suit greets you on the showroom floor and begins explaining how foolish you'd be to pass up the deal. You ask him why the price is so low, and he says,

> Like I said, this thing's fully loaded. Oh, there is one tiny little problem. That stupid manufacturer forgot to install the steering mechanism. But once you get this baby out on a straight open stretch, you'll fall in love. Want leather seats?

What's true for a car is true for solving a conflict problem. Even after we've picked a direction, we still have to steer it. Without steering, a car won't reach its destination and a problem won't reach its resolution.

Answering this fifth question enables us to adjust the structure we've implemented if and when it's necessary. If we don't, we're likely to conclude, "We tried but it didn't work. What's the use?" Bad conflict reemerges, resignation sets in, and the problem doesn't get solved after all.

When Neil and Laura Evaluated Their Solution

Neil and Laura resolved their difference with a win–win solution and laid out specific steps to implement it. So far, so good. But nothing was ever that easy with Kevin. He had mastered the art of derailing things, so Neil and Laura figured they'd better expect the unexpected. Keven would probably agree with the plan for now only to sabotage it later. So Neil and Laura built in some checkpoints to see if their solution was being implemented. As predicted, it usually wasn't. For instance, they discovered during their first inspection that Kevin's paychecks were being deposited not in the bank but under his bed with the dust bunnies and fast-food wrappers.

A tweaking of the plan was in order. They had Kevin arrange for his paychecks to be direct-deposited so that the balance could be monitored regularly. Neil and Laura had a good plan, but if they didn't check it and make adjustments along the way, it would never work.

Next summer would arrive with no money saved, and they'd be facing the same problem.

To answer this question, "When will we evaluate it?" Neil and Laura used their responsibility muscles, which enabled them to see what wasn't working and feel bothered enough to make the needed changes.

Conflict problems can't be fixed without answering all five of the questions. That may take us 3 hours, 3 minutes, or 30 seconds, but leaving any of them unanswered means the problem won't get fixed.

1. Which problem are we trying to fix? If we argue about everything instead of focusing on one thing, we'll get nowhere.

2. Why do we feel so strongly? If we don't understand and validate each other's positions, our arguments will become battles over whose preferences have the greater validity.

3. How can we agree to fix this? If we don't settle on mutual solutions, the conversations will end with no solution at all.

4. What will we do to implement it? If we don't structure a way to implement our solutions, they won't come to pass.

5. When will we evaluate it? If we fail to steer when needed, we'll experience futility, which lends to frustration and the belief that we'll never solve the conflict problem.

Neil and Laura's Process

Over the last three chapters, we've seen how Neil and Laura changed conflict systems. Before they did this, any problem—big or small—could trigger their reaction cycle. Consequently, nothing was ever solved, their home atmosphere felt increasingly awful, they were growing apart, and they were becoming worse and worse versions of themselves.

Because of space constraints in relating their story, it may seem like the change was quick. It wasn't. Neil and Laura's conflict transformation wasn't simple, quick, or easy. They worked hard, it took a while, they often wanted to throw in the towel, it was a lot more difficult than they thought it would be, and both wondered frequently if things would ever change.

But they did change. We'll probably not see them on an infomercial gazing rapturously into each other's eyes, thinking each other's thoughts, or holding hands while skipping merrily down the beach. What they do have is a *real* relationship. They still argue the old way at times, but now they are more likely to turn the conflict around and solve things, so they can forget what they argued about. Their conflict solutions range from win–wins to impasses, but they work them out together. As a result of all this, they've started liking each other again and seem to be getting closer. Neil's better self shows up more often and so does Laura's. At first their conflict system felt awful to them and to me. So it felt wonderful to all three of us when they pulled off a regime change—they overthrew their old system of bad conflict and replaced it with a new government of good conflict.

One More Thing—It Might Be You

We've been discussing the interactive effects of button pushing and reacting. But maybe your contributions to the bad conflict cycle seem disproportionate. Your buttons are exceptionally sensitized, your reactions are nuclear, or you frequently hear people using the term "shock and awe" to describe how you push buttons. If the cause has more to do with you as an individual than it does with the relationship, then the solution will be more personal than relational. You may need some help understanding what's behind your lopsided contributions. Getting help when it's needed is not a sign of weakness and craziness but of strength and sanity.

The following chart summarizes the five crucial questions to ask for good conflict resolution.

5 Crucial Questions for Good Conflict

Question	Action Needed	Muscle Needed	If Unanswered
Which problem will we fix?	Focus on fixing one problem at a time	Awareness	You argue about everything so nothing gets fixed
Why do we feel so strongly?	Validate each other's views	Empathy	You argue over whose preferences have the greater validity
How can we agree to fix this?	Pick a solution that satisfies the interests of both sides (5 options)	Humility	You argue but never agree on a way to fix it
What will we do to implement it?	Define solution in specific terms	Reliability	You argue over the same problem again and again
When will we evaluate it?	Adjust the structure when necessary	Responsibility	You conclude problem fixing doesn't work

In a Nutshell

There are five questions that must be answered for a conflict problem to be fixed. We must address problems one at a time, understand each other's interests, pick a solution that comes closest to satisfying both sets of interests, ensure that our solution gets implemented, and adjust it when needed so that it comes to pass. Not answering all of these questions means the conflict problem will remain.

For Reflection

1. What results when we argue about multiple problems simultaneously?

2. Name four types of conflict problems. Which ones are most common for you?

3. Why is validation essential in solving a conflict problem? What does it mean? What does it not mean?

4. What are the five questions that must be answered to effectively solve a conflict problem?

5. Name the five solution options. Is one of these best?

6. Explain "agreeing to disagree agreeably."

7. What is meant by the phrase "elephant in the living room"?

8. How are the "reason muscles" discussed in Chapter 3 involved in the process of fixing a conflict problem?

DEALING WITH THE UNREASONABLE

In the small town of Bedford Falls, there was a family man and upstanding citizen named George Bailey. You may recall his name from the popular Christmas film classic *It's a Wonderful Life.* Through a series of misfortunes, George lays aside his dreams of travel and adventure to remain in his hometown, where he begrudgingly runs a lending institution founded by his deceased father. Meanwhile, most of George's high school friends have moved on to fame and fortune elsewhere. But the citizens of Bedford Falls deeply respect George Bailey for his integrity, trustworthiness, and generosity.

George's antagonist is Mr. Potter. Potter is a wretched individual who uses his wealth and influence to gain control of everything in town—except the Bailey Building and Loan. It galls Mr. Potter to no end that he repeatedly fails to wrest control of this institution from the Bailey family. The citizens of Bedford Falls love George Bailey but loathe Mr. Potter.

George is a reasonable person, the kind we talked about in Section 2. He's not perfect but has what it takes to build healthy, lasting friendships, of which he has many. Mr. Potter, on the other hand, exemplifies an unreasonable person whose defects are deep, pervasive, and malignant. Many unreasonable people are charming despite their flaws, but not Mr. Potter. He's a despicable person who is deeply despised by the citizenry.

Because George lives and works with others in close quarters, he has people problems. He learns that the methods used to solve problems with reasonable people are quite different from the ones required to deal with unreasonable people like Mr. Potter.

The concept of good conflict isn't an easy one for us to get our heads around. It's hard enough when our conflict opponents are reasonable people who have the ability and willingness to work through the differences. But what about people like Mr. Potter? How do we handle jerks at work, high-maintenance folks at church, relatives we wish would move overseas, and other difficult people? The principles in Section 2 that work so well with reasonable people don't work with unreasonable people, so what different methods can we employ?

As we explore different methods, I'll introduce you to Patti, a frustrated participant in what might be called a "momma drama." The unreasonable person in her life was her own mother. Patti had been trying to handle her mom by employing all she knew about conflict with reasonable people, but nothing was working. In the coming chapters we'll examine how Patti changed bad conflict into good conflict with someone who had no ability to work through differences in a healthy way.

If you are currently at your wit's end trying to handle an unreasonable person, read on!

The Story of Patti

Patti was pleasant when we first met but also seemed apprehensive, this being her first ever visit with a mental health professional. She made several nervous jokes about being "crazy" and asked kiddingly if she was supposed to lie down on the couch for analysis. Hoping to ease her fears, I joked around a bit and tried to be reassuring. I told her that the real crazies of the world don't usually come into offices like mine. Though she was ill at ease, I could tell she was really hoping to get some help.

I asked her to explain her reasons for coming. She elaborated on how she felt overwhelmed all the time, especially by the demands of being a wife and mom. Patti had been married for eight years to her husband, Bill, and they had a five-year-old boy and a two-year-old girl. She felt she was doing a bad job of being a wife and an even worse job of being a mother. The more she talked about her day-to-day life, the clearer it became just how much she was hurting. Her friends had commented on it, Bill had noticed it, and she even found herself identifying with one of those TV ads on depression because it sounded so much like her.

After giving me the synopsis, she smiled and inquired, "So, can you fix me?" Contained in this question was a not-so-subtle demand for psychological twinkle dust that would make her pain instantly disappear. I told her I couldn't promise a quick fix, but our working together would help her eventually feel better—if we could do a good job of finding and addressing the causes of her depression. The work would likely be hard at times, but it would be doable and definitely worth the effort. This wasn't exactly the twinkle dust answer she hoped for, but she agreed to hear more about the process.

I asked Patti if there were other things causing stress besides the daily demands of wifehood and motherdom. She responded dismissively, "Oh, well, my mother is driving me nuts, but what else is new, right? Other than that, I can't think of anything."

She then told me that her parents had divorced shortly after she and Bill married, and her mother had moved to the same city to be closer to them. I asked her to explain the phrase "my mother is driving me nuts."

She gave me quite a list. Her mom calls several times a day, expects to visit with them several times a week, frequently asks for favors, drops in unexpectedly, and she gets upset if they let anyone else babysit. Patti then said, "I don't really understand this, but she almost seems jealous of my relationship with Bill and the kids. She gets upset if I ever do something with just my family. It's almost like she's competing with them for my attention."

Then, as if hit by a sudden wave of remorse, Patti said, "I don't mean to sit here and criticize my mom though. She's really sweet and will do anything for us. We're really lucky to have her so close by." She then smiled, folded her arms, and said, "Hey, I've always heard that shrinks try to get you to blame everything on your parents. Are you wanting me to become a mom basher?"

I laughed because I was so tickled by her directness, and I assured her that parent-bashing would not be our therapeutic objective.

Relieved, she said, "Good, just checking."

And I really meant what I said—this would not become a "blame the parents" quest. And yet it was my clear impression that Patti was exceptionally sensitive about the mom subject, which I decided to drop for the moment. We spent the next session or two discussing her history and background.

Patti grew up in one of those small towns where the streetlights dim when someone plugs in a hair dryer. She was the oldest of two children, her brother being two years younger. Her dad was a local businessman, sort of a big fish in a small pond. Her mom worked part-time in one of husband's businesses but had mostly stayed home to raise the kids. Patti described her early years as idyllic. She and her friends rode bikes, played in the fields nearby, waded in the creek that ran through their property, caught fireflies in the summer, and had snowball fights in the winter.

But troubles lurked beneath this facade of All-American life. Dad was an alcoholic, but not a good-natured one. He was a mean drunk, saying and doing abusive things to his wife and children during his drinking episodes. No one outside the family ever saw this side of Patti's dad. If he was late to work, that was his prerogative as the business owner. He served on several local boards and was an elder in their church. There was a huge discrepancy between how he was perceived by the public and who he actually was in private.

Patti's mom had her own discrepancies. Sometimes she was like Betty Crocker, the domestic and cheerful homemaker. At other times she was dark and brooding like Bette Davis in her "evil vixen" movie roles. This drove Patti crazy because she never knew whether she'd encounter Betty or Bette when she got home, which is probably why she spent so much time outside playing with her friends.

And then there was her brother, Phil, who was the "black sheep" of the family. He didn't have discrepancies; he was consistently a jerk. Patti didn't go into a lot of detail about Phil, but I got the picture. He was a problem at home and a problem at school. He prided himself on his alternative appearance and did all he could to resist family expectations. Much of the family energy was channeled in Phil's direction.

It was clear all along that two systems governed the household. There was the "Dad system" that kicked in when Dad was present and the "Mom system" that ruled most of the time because Dad was seldom there. Patti often found herself navigating the difficult terrain of maintaining allegiance to one without offending the other. Home was a minefield where the smallest of missteps might blow off a leg.

As Patti grew older, Mom increasingly confided in her about the struggles she experienced with Dad and Phil. An oft-repeated phrase was "Us girls have to stick together." Usually it was unclear who was parenting whom. Mom would ask Patti's advice about how to handle Phil, and then get mad if her suggestions failed. She unburdened herself by disclosing her most personal struggles with Patti's dad, including details about their sex life. Even back then Patti understood how terribly inappropriate this was, but she couldn't figure out how to sidestep the information dump.

While Phil was the black sheep, Patti was the responsible child who seldom caused any trouble, made good grades, and represented the family well in the community. She graduated in the top 10 percent of her class and went to college, where she made lots of friends and continued to excel. During her college years, Mom and Dad separated. Phil dropped out of school and moved into a ratty rental house with some guys who drank a lot and barely supported themselves with low-paying, part-time jobs. The once idyllic picture had morphed into an ugly portrait of gloom and tragedy. For Patti, being away at college was like sitting on a perch overlooking her family's dysfunction. She had a bird's eye view. She was sad about her family and, at the same time, very glad to be away.

In the last two years of college Patti met and steadily dated Bill, a good guy. During their courtship, Patti was struck with an unpleasant realization. She became conscious of just how much her mom was still "inside her head." Patti's mom had a terribly negative view of men, which was understandable given that she was the daughter of an alcoholic, she married an abusive alcoholic, and her son was rapidly becoming a shiftless bum. Patti discovered that she had unwittingly internalized this negative image through dozens, if not hundreds, of "girl talks," in which Mom portrayed men as caveman-like figures whose knuckles dragged the ground. Consequently, Patti's starting point assumptions about Bill were colored by these deeply imbedded conceptions. Over time, however, the picture that emerged of Bill simply didn't line up with the internalized image. Sure, he had foibles just like anyone else, but he was not the ghastly troll that Patti's mom had coached her to expect. This made Patti realize the importance of distinguishing between her thoughts and her mom's thoughts and the necessity of forming her own opinions—even if they differed from her mom's.

When she and Bill graduated, married, and started their new lives together, Patti assumed she'd left behind the negatives of the past. They were forming a good marriage, had great jobs, and, after a while, began a family. Jason was born three years into the marriage, and Megan came along three years later. Just after Jason was born, Patti's mom and dad's separation culminated in a divorce. Not wanting to remain in that small town, Mom picked up and moved to where Patti and Bill lived so she could "be close to family and help with babysitting."

Patti was flooded with mixed feelings about Mom's geographical relocation. On the one hand Mom had some wonderful positives, and Patti relished the idea of her kids growing up with their grandmother close by. On the other hand, living in such close proximity to Mom's negatives left her feeling very apprehensive.

As it turned out, Patti's fears had validity. Even though Mom lived several miles away, she occupied a place at the center of their lives, with most things revolving around her needs, her preferences, and her schedule. Patti often referred to her mom as their "third child" because the amount of attention she demanded rivaled that required by her own children. It was always all about Mom. Patti spewed like an unplugged fire hydrant when I asked her to give me some examples. Here are some snippets of what she told me over the next few weeks:

- "She's always expecting us to drop what we're doing and cater to her every need. She gets hurt or mad if we don't. I feel guilt-tripped all the time, like I'm being selfish if I don't make what's going on with her the center of my universe."

- "In some ways, it's always been like this. When she couldn't figure out what to do with Phil, she came to me for advice— like I would know what to do. When Dad went into one of his drunken tirades, she relied on me to help her through it. She's always leaned on me, and she's leaning now harder than ever."

- "Mom has this mysterious, nonspecific medical condition that I can't ever pin down, no matter how many times I ask. I can't tell you the number of times Bill or I have had to rearrange our schedules to transport her to the doctor or pick up a prescription at some inopportune time. I hate to say this about my own mother, but we've wondered if she's even sick at all. She's able to go anywhere or do anything when it's important to her, but at other times she supposedly can't make it without our assistance."

- "I'm not the biggest fan of Alexander Graham Bell. I've gotten to where I hate to hear the phone ring because I know it's going to be Mom on the other end, whining and complaining about something that's gone wrong or someone who's done her wrong. You know, that wouldn't bother me so much if she were open to solutions. But whenever I offer suggestions that would actually solve one of those problems, she quickly informs me that I can't possibly understand since everything in my life is so 'perfect.' Sometimes I think she enjoys her misery."

- "The thing is, I like helping people. I do volunteer work

and enjoy assisting people in need. But the help we provide for Mom is never enough, like it drops into a bottomless pit. This sounds awful, but I help her because I have to, not because I want to. We've tried politely declining, but she has this way of making us feel like we're being selfish if we refuse to help."

• "Here's another thing that drives me crazy. Bill's always treated Mom with respect. But I can't tell you how many times she's made negative remarks about him—nothing blatantly ugly but always quietly disparaging. And when we're all together, she talks only to me, treating him as if he's invisible. It offends him, but it's really offensive to me as well."

I asked Patti to describe the typical way she and Bill end up in the helping role. She said,

> OK, here's a typical scenario. Bill, the kids, and I had been out for a while last week, and our message light was blinking when we came in. There were six messages from Mom, each one sounding more frantic than the one before. She needed this particular prescription from the pharmacy and was panicked about what would happen if she didn't get it. Mom drives and the drugstore is right down the road from her house. She could easily have gotten it herself. Yet if we didn't drive the 13 miles to her neighborhood and pick up the prescription, her health would suffer, and it would somehow be our fault. That's the sort of thing that happens all the time.

Even though I already knew the answer, I asked if she'd ever tried talking to her mom about the things that bothered her. She said, "Are you kidding? Like a gazillion times. But trying to work things out with her is like slamming my head over and over into a wall. Nothing makes the slightest difference, no matter what I say or how I say it." Hoping to get a better feel for what happens when conflict occurs, I asked her to tell me more about that "slamming my head over and over into a wall" remark:

- "The more we argue, the worse she gets and the more frustrated I become. I can't imagine her ever backing down about anything. I'd rather lie down in an ant bed than have an argument with her."

- "Mom never admits to being wrong about anything, even when she's clearly in the wrong. She's irritatingly oblivious to the faults that others so clearly see. She never apologizes for anything because, to hear her tell it, she never does anything wrong."

- "Arguments with Mom confuse me and mess with my brain. On the one hand, I see what she does and know it's legitimate to feel angry at her. But I usually end up feeling guilty for my anger, figuring that the difficulties we experience are somehow my fault."

After hearing the abridged version of a very long tale, it was evident to me that Patti was experiencing "momma drama trauma." Yes, she was depressed, but her depression resulted from momma drama participation, and her ongoing involvement was continuing to feed it. I explained that she would probably stay depressed unless Mom moved to New Guinea or Patti developed ways of avoiding participation in the dramas that were continuously being staged by her mother.

Patti had that look on her face that a person has when a dentist explains root canals. She told me I'd merely confirmed what she'd known all along, but she still wasn't looking forward to the process. In fact, a root canal seemed more appealing than doing what was necessary to alter the mom/daughter relationship. But momma drama was now occupying the center stage of her life, while her other commitments, such as marriage and motherhood, were being neglected. She wasn't looking forward to dealing with her mom, but she knew it was necessary to change conflict systems—from bad to good.

Chapter 6

ASSESSING THE OPPOSITION

*Insane people are always sure they are fine.
It is only the sane people who are willing
to admit that they are crazy.*
NORA EPHRON

*The words of a fool start fights;
do him a favor and gag him.*
PROVERBS 18:6

Have you dealt with someone who seems so unreasonable that you ask, "Hey, what's up with that guy?" In this chapter we're going to take a look at how people like Mr. Potter and Patti's mom are wired and what makes them tick. Then we'll examine how to accurately assess the unreasonable person so we can deal with him or her effectively. Conflict with unreasonable people goes well only when we first know and understand what we're up against.

Unreasonable People Are Everywhere

Unreasonable people are called many things. Several of the terms contain swear words, refer to body parts, or deliberately insult the person's ancestry. We've all heard them, and most of us have used them on occasion. The list that follows is by no means exhaustive but includes some of the common terms, omitting the more tasteless ones.

big baby	loon	prima donna
bull in a china shop	loony bird	psycho
bully	loser	schmuck
control freak	martyr	smooth operator
crazy-maker	messiah	snake in the grass
creep	moron	turkey
drama queen	nut	victim
freak show	nut case	wacko
guilt tripper	pain in the neck	weasel
horse's tail	personality disorder	wolf in sheep's
jerk	piece of work	clothing

If unreasonable people are despotic rulers of nations, we call them "mad men." In the Bible, they are called "fools" or "the wicked." Unfortunately, we encounter unreasonable people throughout life. They first show up as toddlers throwing temper tantrums. At that point, the unreasonable person is a kid who needs to mature—to develop better ways of handling frustration. The ones who don't mature (for various reasons) show up again in elementary school as bullies on the playground. Again, the need is to grow—to learn more mature ways of dealing with peers. Those who fail to mature become adults who are called the names just mentioned. The unreasonable person is a child in an adult's body, a person who needs to grow up—to learn more mature ways of handling relationships and conflict.

Unreasonable people truly are everywhere, and a large percentage of the population meets the criteria we'll be discussing. We run into them at work, at school, at church, in the community, at the doctor's office, in government, in entertainment, at family gatherings, and in marriages. In fact, there are sleeper cells of unreasonable people all over the place. The following descriptive phrases are commonly used in reference to unreasonable people:

arrogant	going mental	repugnant
audacious	high maintenance	self-important
complex	high schoolish	sick
confusing	insecure	slimy
crazy	insufferable	stubborn
crazy as a loon	irritating	toxic
difficult	loony	treacherous
disordered	manipulative	two-faced
ego-centric	narcissistic	wacked
full of it	psychotic	

Joyce Landorf Heatherly referred to unreasonable people as "irregular."[1] Susan Forward refers to them as "emotional blackmailers."[2] Henry Cloud and John Townsend call them "unsafe."[3] Scott Peck refers to them as "evil."[4] Sometimes the word "political" is used, usually in a pejorative sense, communicating the idea that the people are two-faced, back-biting, power-hungry, self-advancing, conniving, and duplicitous. Hence, someone will say, "I didn't want to be on that board because it's so political." Jimmy Stewart, who played the title character in another Frank Capra film, *Mr. Smith Goes to Washington*, encountered the worst form of politics when he arrived in the nation's capital. Patriotism had attracted him to the nobility of public service, but he was depressingly disillusioned after discovering that some of his most idealized heroes were drastically different people in private than what they appeared to be in public—one of the chief characteristics of unreasonable people.

We are simultaneously fascinated by and frustrated with unreasonable people. We make movies about them, write books about them, and keep up with them through the tabloids. They are often people with dazzling positives alongside glaring negatives, and it's that mix of opposing traits that makes them so interesting and confounding. We often make one or more of the following statements about an unreasonable person:

- He has some screws loose.
- She thinks the world revolves around her.
- She'll stab you in the back.
- He creeps me out.
- She wears me out.
- There's one in every crowd.
- She's never wrong about anything.
- When she fights, she shows her true colors.
- He gives me the heebie jeebies.
- Here comes Joe, hide!
- Once you're on her bad side, you can't get back.
- He's always got an angle.
- She thinks everyone's out to get her.
- She sucks all the air out of the room.
- He thinks the rules don't apply to him.
- Being around her is a real soap opera.
- Joe's wife has got to be a saint.

Unreasonable People Haven't Grown Up

The house I grew up in was next to a neighborhood park, and one of my playmates, Hector, lived across the field. He and I would play in the park with other kids from the neighborhood. Several things stand out in my memories about Hector. First, I had never known anyone else with that name. Second, he always wore the same pair of dirty, untied tennis shoes. Third, he drooled a lot and wiped it with a handkerchief his mom had given him. Finally, he was always smiling, and we had lots of fun.

This story probably makes you feel good if it conjures up pleasant memories from your own childhood. But I left out an important piece of information. Hector was in his twenties back then. He had a condition that left him mentally and physically impaired. His shoes were untied because he couldn't tie them. He drooled because he was unable to control his saliva. He was happy playing with little children because his own mental development had stalled at the level of a small child.

Now how do you feel about the story? Hector, it turns out, was chronologically old but developmentally young. It's tragic when a discrepancy exists between the two.

Unreasonable people have that sort of discrepancy. While it's true that everyone has maturity gaps, unreasonable people have pervasive impairments in their abilities to handle people problems. Some of the parts that are needed to flex and adjust in conflict situations didn't develop along with the rest of the parts, leaving them inflexible and rigid, lacking the "give and take" possessed by reasonable people. They are grown-ups who haven't grown up.

Why They Stopped Growing

Frequently a reasonable person being driven crazy by an unreasonable person will ask me, "What do you think is wrong with him?" That's hard to say. The problem could have an internal cause, such as something genetic or a brain malfunction that developed later in life (nature). Or it could have to do with external factors, such as having a deficient upbringing (nurture). Or it could be the result of his choices (what he's done with nature and nurture). Often it's a combination of factors. For whatever reason, the unreasonable person passed up or missed opportunities to grow up, becoming chronologically older while remaining developmentally young. He or she is now a child in a grown-up's body.

What Stopped Growing

In Chapter 3 we discussed the "reason muscles," which are what we need to use to do the right things with personal wrongness. Reasonable people have these muscles, which become stronger with use. If two reasonable people argue and handle their flaws well, they are likely to reach a resolution. Unreasonable people don't have some or all of these muscles. They never developed them, or they've become atrophied from years of disuse.

Unreasonable people have an aversion to personal wrongness that extends far beyond anything experienced by reasonable people. To them, being wrong presents a threat to survival that equals most physical threats. Unreasonable people put all of their energy into safeguarding rightness—to staying safe—and none into solving conflict problems. They're not interested in solving problems if doing so requires the acknowledgment of wrongness.

Let's look at the five "reason muscles" and what they look like in unreasonable people. Remember, having these muscles and using them is what distinguishes a reasonable person from someone who is not.

The Humility Muscle

The first muscle needed to handle wrongness well is the *humility* muscle, which gives a person the ability to acknowledge potential personal wrongness. When reasonable people use this muscle, the stance is, "I could be wrong, you could be right, let's talk." Reasonable people, who have healthy humility muscles, can handle being wrong if being right requires sacrificing the truth. They believe, though perhaps reluctantly, in the maxim, "Truth is your best ally." It may be painful to acknowledge wrongness, but they'll do so because being truthful has a higher value to them than being right.

Unwilling to allow for the possibility of wrongness, unreasonable people will sacrifice truth if being truthful means being wrong. They'll even lie to avoid being wrong. In fact, some unreasonable people revise truth so routinely that they delude themselves and come to believe their own revisions. The stance taken is, "I'm right, you're wrong, end of discussion." They can be arrogant and inflexible. That's why you can't reason with them. Your attempts at reasonableness won't work because they're not interested in reason; they're only interested in winning or in being right.

The Awareness Muscle

The second muscle needed is the *awareness* muscle, which enables us to observe areas of actual personal wrongness. Having this muscle, the reasonable person's stance is, "I see where I'm wrong." They see their strengths but also understand their weaknesses. Unreasonable people have ruled out the possibility of wrongness, so the stance taken is, "I only see where I'm right." Unreasonable people are notoriously lacking in self-awareness, not seeing the flaws in themselves that others so clearly see. Therefore, when problems occur, they automatically assume that others caused them.

In Chapter 3 we talked about press boxes and mirrors. The press box is the part of our personalities that enables us to make big-picture self-observations. For unreasonable people, the wires connecting the press box to the sidelines phones are severed. They don't have press box conversations and are sorely lacking in awareness. That's why we say:

- She has no idea how she comes across.
- He's a bull in a china shop.
- He's clueless about the part he played in that argument.
- Her husband sees it, her kids see it, her boss sees it. Everybody sees it but her.
- She's oblivious.

Relationships are like mirrors in which we catch glimpses of the good and bad parts of ourselves. Reasonable people make use of the feedback that relationships provide. But unreasonable people catch no reflections of their flaws in relational mirrors.

The Responsibility Muscle

Sometimes referred to as a conscience, the *responsibility* muscle enables us to be bothered by personal wrongness. Unreasonable people are weak in the conscience department. While the reasonable person observes personal faults and cringes, the unreasonable person shrugs when flaws are pointed out. His or her stance is, "If I'm wrong, so what?"

One Sunday afternoon I sat riveted to a documentary about a well-known American who was great in public but not so great in private. With the passage of time, his once-concealed infidelities have become part of the historical record. A family friend was interviewed who recounted a conversation in which she asked him why he would take such chances and jeopardize his legacy. In response he calmly replied, "I guess I just can't help it." She then made this astute observation:

> He always lived his life in compartments. There was the public compartment, in which he accomplished these great things, all of which were true. But he also had an unseen compartment in which he was repeatedly unfaithful to his wife and children. I think he knew there were discrepancies between the compartments, but they just didn't bother him that much.

In effect, the unreasonable person looks in the mirror, sees the glob of spinach on his teeth, doesn't like what he sees, and decides to quit looking in mirrors. The reasonable person *seeks* out truth to change for the better. The unreasonable person *runs* from truth to avoid discomfort.

The Empathy Muscle

The fourth muscle needed is the *empathy* muscle. Empathy is the ability to be bothered if our personal wrongness hurts others. It enables us to understand the effects we have on the other person and to use that understanding to govern our words and actions.

When a reasonable person uses this muscle, the resulting stance is, "It bothers me when my wrongness hurts you." He allows that understanding to shape how he behaves toward others. The unreasonable person is empathy deficient. His stance is, "I'm only bothered when your wrongness hurts me." Consequently, the unreasonable person is often described as "cruel" or "insensitive" in his dealings with others. That's why we say, "It's all about him" or "I can't believe she could say (or do) that" or "Watch out, he'll stab you in the back." The unreasonable person gives little consideration to the impact of his words and actions on others. Reciprocal empathy is a realistic expectation in conflict with reasonable people. With unreasonable people, however, we should anticipate self-serving motivation and behaviors.

The Reliability Muscle

The *reliability* muscle is the ability to correct personal wrongness. A reasonable person is bothered by his flaws and determines, "When I'm wrong, I'll change." Since the unreasonable person fails to see his flaws, he is neither bothered by them nor sees the need to correct them. Consequently, his stance is, "I'll not change because I'm not wrong."

Prof. Howard Hendricks notes that people have two types of needs: *real needs* and *felt needs*.[5] A real need must be felt before we'll do anything about it. For instance, you could have cancer but not know it—an undetected but very real malady that needs attention. If your doctor diagnosed it, you'd become aware of the illness, feel the need, and seek treatment. Evaluation and diagnosis would transform your real need into a felt need. Unreasonable people have flaws but don't see them, so they do nothing to correct them. Frequently a client being driven crazy by an unreasonable person remarks, "He's the one who really needs to be in here getting help." That may be true, but no one seeks help without first realizing help is needed. The unreasonable person doesn't see that anything is wrong with him, so why should he seek help? Change presupposes awareness.

That's why the Mr. Potters of the world rarely come to offices like mine—they believe there's nothing wrong with them. In *It's a Wonderful Life*, Mr. Potter saw himself as the good guy, the smart and powerful person looking after lazy and uneducated townsfolk. Having that view of himself, why would he ever change anything?

So here's what we're up against when we have conflict with unreasonable people. They automatically assume we're the ones in the wrong, they fail to see their contributions to the conflict, they claim no responsibility for any part of the problem, they're not bothered by the impact of their words and actions on us, and they change nothing because nothing about them needs changing. Is it any wonder that unreasonable people are so difficult for us to handle?

This chart summarizes the different outcomes when the "reason muscles" are used by reasonable people and not used by unreasonable people.

Outcomes of Reason Muscle Use

Reason Muscle	When Used (Reasonable People)	When Not Used (Unreasonable People)
Humility	I could be wrong, you could be right, let's talk	I'm right, you're wrong, end of discussion
Awareness	I see where I'm wrong	I only see where I'm right
Responsibility	It bothers me when I'm wrong	If I'm wrong, so what?
Empathy	It bothers me when my wrongness hurts you	I'm only bothered when your wrongness hurts me
Reliability	When I'm wrong, I'll change	I'll not change because I'm not wrong

The Unreasonable Person's Conflict Goal

When two reasonable people argue, their buttons get pushed, they react, they push buttons, they fail to use their "reason muscles," they make mistakes, and it may look and sound pretty ugly. But ultimately they are heading for the same objective: solving the problem. When a reasonable person argues with an unreasonable person, they have different objectives. The reasonable person's conflict goal is resolution while the unreasonable person's goal is rightness.

My two oldest children are girls born three years apart. They are both now extremely articulate, but when the youngest was first learning to talk, she was consistently out chattered by her loquacious older sister. Realizing her verbal disadvantage, the youngest would start swinging her fists. She hoped to accomplish physically what couldn't be accomplished verbally.

Similarly, an unreasonable person in conflict with a reasonable person is at a disadvantage because he's fighting someone who has something he doesn't possess—"reason muscles." He lacks what's necessary to do the right things with the wrongness. Therefore, he opts for a different conflict goal—rightness—which requires no wrongness acknowledgment. When the dust settles, he doesn't care about mutually satisfying problem solutions, but he does care about being right. To the unreasonable person, being right is entwined with his identity as a person and/or survival.[6] He needs to eat, he needs to breathe, and he needs to be right.

The Unreasonable Person's Means of Reaching the Goal: Drama

Unable and/or unwilling to tolerate wrongness, the unreasonable person opts for the only acceptable conflict outcome to him or her—rightness—and the method used to achieve that outcome is usually *drama*.[7] For example, suppose you're in a checkout line and the lady in front of you has two-year-old Suzie in her shopping cart. Suzie begs for something off the rack close to the register, and mom says no. Suzie asks again. Mom says no again. Suzie begs louder. Mom says no louder. Customers six aisles away have now joined you as members of the audience. The power struggle escalates to a crescendo until finally…guess what happens. Mom gives in. Suzie wins. Suzie's agitation drops considerably while Mom's agitation spikes through the stratosphere. Suzie is now the calm, good guy in control. Mom is now the exasperated bad guy who's out of control.

Lacking the maturity to reason, Suzie has just staged *a drama* to get what she wants and wins without using any "reason muscles." When toddlers do this, we call them spoiled brats. When adolescents do this, we call them bullies. When adults do this, we call them unreasonable people, jerks, and any of the myriad other names we come up with. In fact, dealing with an adult unreasonable person is very much like dealing with a child throwing a temper tantrum.

Some unreasonable people are openly dramatic, the kind we refer to as "drama queens" (or "drama kings") while others stage dramas in ways that are almost undetectable. Most unreasonable people missed attending Good Conflict Camp, but they all attended Drama School, where they developed into thespians of the highest order. That's why certain terms have become associated with unreasonable people: theatrics, grand-standing, mind games, soap operas.

I'm sometimes asked, "Do they know what they're doing? Do they plan out these dramas deliberately?" Good question. It's less likely that they plan them and more likely that drama has been used so routinely that it's done without conscious deliberation. Perhaps some people do both. Many unreasonable people seem to get so caught up in their drama that they lose the ability to distinguish between drama and real life.

Drama's Purpose

On March 4, 1933, Franklin Roosevelt was about to be inaugurated as president of the United States during one of the nation's most difficult periods, the Great Depression. In his thirties Roosevelt was stricken with polio, rendering his leg muscles useless. Having to rely exclusively on his arms, he developed enormous upper body strength. Leg braces, which could be locked into place, enabled him to stand upright when giving speeches.

Roosevelt knew the populace was demoralized and needed leadership that was strong, visionary, and courageous. He also understood that the picture of a president taking the oath of office from a wheelchair would not inspire confidence in a day when most people doubted the capabilities of disabled individuals. These images would be broadcast to a depressed nation using the newly developed media of the day—"talkies" or motion pictures with sound.

So Roosevelt devised a plan. After being discreetly helped from his chair, he used his powerful arms to brace himself on the arms of men on either side as they all made their way to the front. They had carefully choreographed, paced, and timed their movements in such a way that Roosevelt appeared to be walking with the group. In reality, his legs only lightly brushed the floor as he was carried along. His braces were locked into place at the podium, and he took the oath of office. To a beleaguered nation, he stood and delivered his inaugural address, which contained the confidence-inspiring line, "The only thing we have to fear is fear itself."

Here's my point. Roosevelt had atrophied muscles that were incapable of use and, had this knowledge been revealed, his leadership and survival as president would likely have been jeopardized. Therefore, he learned to act strong in places where he was actually weak. The strategy worked. And that's what the unreasonable person does. He has atrophied "reason muscles" and, if this were revealed, he'd have to admit wrongness, something he's unwilling to face because it threatens his survival. He uses drama to act strong where he is actually weak. Roosevelt performed his drama for a noble purpose—to provide strong national leadership. The unreasonable person performs his drama for self-serving reasons—to maintain rightness and avoid wrongness.

Drama's Operation

The drama is staged to give the unreasonable person an opportunity to play the role of good guy, the guy who is in the right. We'll look at four good-guy roles the unreasonable person performs: master, messiah, martyr, and mute. To be certain, there are other roles unreasonable people play, but these are common ones. We'll also examine how the drama unfolds through three acts: enticement, enlistment, and establishment.

Roles

The first good-guy role we'll examine is the *master*. The stance is, "I'll be in charge because somebody's got to do it." The master has to be in control. We describe masters using terms and phrases such as "He's a control freak," "He's got to be in charge," "Everything has to be her way," "It's his way or the highway," "He micromanages everything," "She has control issues."

Psychology professor Emeritus Sheldon Cashdan refers to this as a need for power and states, "The overall purpose...is to create a relationship where the recipient is forced to take a subservient role."[8] The toddler throwing a temper tantrum has a need for power. When the drama concludes, she's in charge. The bully on the playground uses drama to accomplish the same purpose. In a similar fashion, some adults stage power dramas to be in control.

The second good-guy role is *messiah*. "I sacrifice to help people" is the stance taken. We describe them as rescuer, caretaker, knight in shining armor, brown noser, know it all, God's gift to the world, and needs to be needed. Cashdan refers to this as ingratiation and says, "Relationships are orchestrated so that others are constantly aware that the person...is giving up something or putting the recipient's interests before his own. There is a concerted attempt to induce others to be grateful for the things one does and the sacrifices one makes."[9] Eddie Haskell from the old TV show *Leave It to Beaver* was this type of unreasonable person. He was a nasty jerk. But around Mr. and Mrs. Cleaver, he quickly slipped into the messiah role, saying, "My, that's a beautiful dress, Mrs. Cleaver" or "Don't worry, Mr. Cleaver. I'll make sure little Theodore stays out of trouble when Wally and I take him to the malt shop this afternoon."

Webster defines the third role, *martyr*, as "great or constant sufferer." The good-guy role played by the martyr is, "I've been hurt, and you should feel sorry for me. By the way, it will be your fault if I don't make it." We describe these folks using terms such as guilt tripper, victim, help-rejecting complainer, and dependent. Speaking of this dependency, Cashdan says, "Such individuals are convinced that the success of their relationships, particularly close ones, hinges on their ability to convince people that they cannot exist on their own. They consequently adopt the emotional demeanor of a child and coerce (induce) those about them into taking care of them."[10] This illustrates what happens in a martyr drama.

Suppose you and a friend are on a footbridge. Your friend hands you one end of a rope and throws the other end over the railing of the bridge. While you struggle to hold on, he climbs over the railing and down the rope, where he dangles just above the rapids. He hollers up to you, "If you let go of the rope I'll die, and it will be your fault. I'm counting on you to pull me up." Your friend put himself in danger, yet he's now made it your responsibility to save his life.

The last common good-guy role played is the *mute:* "I'm going to get through this conflict by remaining silent and untroubled." When the mute plays his role, we use sentences such as "He's in denial," "We had an argument, and now she acts like nothing happened," "There's this huge elephant in the living room that we can't talk about," "He won't discuss it," "Every time I try to bring up the problem, she changes the subject," and "I'm supposed to just pretend like everything is fine." The mute's role in the drama is to appear untroubled. Our role in the drama is to participate in the pretense. If we don't then we're the troublemaking bad guys who refuse to let things go.

Some unreasonable people fit neatly into these roles. Others aren't so easily categorized and display a combination of features. Or they may play roles that are less common.

The Acts

There are three acts or three parts to the dramas staged by unreasonable people. The first act involves *enticing* the opponent to participate. The second act occurs when the opponent is *enlisted* to perform his role because the drama cannot achieve its purpose without the opponent's participation. The third act occurs when the unreasonable person's good-guy role is *established*. When it's over, he or she takes a bow for a dazzling performance as the one in control, the one who rescues, the one who has been victimized, or the one who is untroubled.

In the movie *It's a Wonderful Life,* Mr. Potter calls George Bailey into his office for a meeting. Mr. Potter, a *master* actor, has devised a scheme for gaining control of the entire town of Bedford Falls. First, Mr. Potter *entices* George's participation. He begins the meeting by voicing many of George's personal misgivings. He describes all of the things George hates about his situation—that he works incredibly long hours, that his high school buddies have moved away and made fortunes elsewhere, and that his job seems like an inescapable trap. Mr. Potter's statements give external expression to many of George's internal thoughts. Concealing his *master* role, Mr. Potter assumes the role of *messiah,* there to liberate George from financial enslavement. He offers George a well-paying job, travel opportunities, and numerous attractive perks. Accepting the offer, of course, will necessitate closing down the Bailey Building and Loan. But he reassures George by saying, "Your ship has just come in."

George's participation has now been *enlisted.* The manipulation works, and George bites the bait. He's so flabbergasted by the large salary proposal that he drops the expensive cigar Mr. Potter had given him. Overwhelmed with gratitude, he asks for time to talk it over with his wife and leans across the desk to shake Mr. Potter's hand. George is now playing his role in the drama: a victim being rescued by the messianic Mr. Potter.

Mr. Potter's role has now been *established.* He comprehended what George had yet to realize. By accepting the proposal, the entire town would fall under Mr. Potter's dictatorial control. Thus far the drama proceeds according to the script. Mr. Potter was ready to take his bow as master, as the good guy in charge of Bedford Falls. Note that Mr. Potter accomplished his purpose, not through reasoning out a solution, but through staging a drama. That's how unreasonable people operate. They establish their roles in the drama by manipulating a person into assuming his or her role.

The Effects of Drama

When the drama succeeds, the unreasonable person feels good and we feel upset. That's because we've been used. He's enticed us into playing the required roles so that he can be the good guy. He's used us to enhance himself. This violation of our boundaries elicits many emotions: rage, exasperation, sadness, anxiety, befuddlement. Concerning these feelings, Scott Peck, who uses the term "evil" for unreasonable people, says,

> The feeling that a healthy person often experiences in relationship with an evil person is revulsion. The feeling of revulsion may be almost instant if the evil encountered is blatant. If the evil is more subtle, the revulsion may develop more gradually as the relationship with the evil one slowly deepens...There is another reaction that the evil frequently engender in us: confusion...Lies confuse.[11]

First, drama participation *makes us sick.* Peck refers to this as "revulsion," and this is why we'll sometimes say, "I just want to throw up" after experiencing the violation. When George Bailey leaned across the desk to shake Mr. Potter's hand, it dawned on him that he'd been scammed. With that realization, he wiped off his hand as if removing a stain. Drama participation makes us feel sick, but it can also make us be sick. The stress involved and the effect on our immune systems can lead to physical illnesses. The phrase "you make me sick" can be literally true.

Second, drama participation *drives us crazy.* Dealing with unreasonable people leaves us confused, baffled, and discombobulated. The purpose of the drama is to obscure the truth by promoting the good-guy lie. As Peck says, "lies confuse," so it stands to reason that getting caught up in the drama has a confusing effect. Here's an illustration of this using an episode of an old TV show called *The Twilight Zone.*

> The setting is a hospital. When the story begins, we see a woman lying in a bed, her face wrapped in bandages. The doctors and nurses appear only in the shadows. The woman had just endured the last in a series of surgical procedures to correct her grotesque appearance. The

doctors expressed little hope for success since all previous surgeries had failed. They encouraged her, instead, to look forward to life in a special colony inhabited by people who were similarly afflicted. If this last-ditch surgical attempt proved unsuccessful, she could be assured of a good life nonetheless.

The anticipated moment arrives for removal of the bandages. When the last dressing falls from her face, a gasp is heard in the background. "It didn't work!" the doctors exclaim. The woman turns and we see her face for the first time. She is ravishingly beautiful. The camera pans the room where the doctors and nurses step out of the shadows. They look like pigs. That's right—humans with pig faces. The woman looks in the mirror, screams with horror at her appearance, and runs down the hallway into the arms of one of her kind—a ruggedly handsome man. The episode ends with these two attractive individuals being escorted away to the ugly people colony.

In this story, pig-faced people had convinced gorgeous people they were hideous. That's what an unreasonable person attempts to do with a reasonable person. His survival depends upon getting us to believe this lie: "I'm OK; you're not." This lie can be so convincing that reasonable people often lose sight of the distinctions between truth and falsehood. One client, who was raised in a family system densely populated with pig-faced, unreasonable people, used this analogy to explain her confusion:

> It became clear to me just how wacked they all were after I had moved away and built healthy relationships with normal people. When I would attend one of the obligatory family gatherings, however, it was so easy for me to lose my perspective. They all truly believed that they were normal and that I was the strange and peculiar one.

I felt like I was in the *Twilight Zone*. It was as though I was standing in front of a red couch commenting to a cousin about the beautiful red color. The cousin would then laugh, exclaiming that the couch was not red but green. Other family members would chime in, laughing hilariously at my colorblindness. I'd leave the gathering thinking to myself, *Maybe it's not red but green like they say. Maybe it's me. Maybe I am color blind. Maybe I'm the peculiar one.* It would take me a while to regain my grasp on reality.

We can feel confused for several reasons. First, there is often a disturbing discrepancy between the public image the unreasonable person portrays and who he or she actually is in private. Attributes, which may be positives in public, are often the same ones that have such a negative effect privately. For instance, a *master* who has to be in charge may excel in commanding a military campaign but be viewed as a controlling jerk at home. Frustratingly, he's lavished with praise for his accomplishments by people who think he's wonderful. And those same people may think something's wrong with us for not agreeing with them. How can someone be such a winner in one realm and simultaneously be such a loser in another? That's confusing.

Second, we may feel confused because the unreasonable person stages dramas on some occasions and not on others. And when they're not staging dramas, they can be very pleasant to be around. For instance, a *messiah* may be happy and normal as long as she is receiving sufficient amounts of gratitude for her caretaking activities. So who is she? The happy normal person or the shrew who makes us feel guilty for failing to appreciate her? That Jekyll and Hyde split is confusing.

Third, the unreasonable person creates a smokescreen by highlighting our flaws and calling us hypocrites for criticizing him. *How dare you judge me when you've got your own shortcomings* is the thought. If successful, we'll think, *Maybe I am being too hard on him. He's right, after all. I do have problems.*

Fourth, he has mastered the art of *projection*. All of us participate in an odd practice developed in the 1920s. We go to large rooms, sit in comfortable chairs, buy incredibly expensive snacks, and stare at a wall for two to three hours. At the end of the time, we leave and discuss the experience with our friends. Often staring at the wall elicits powerful emotions. Why? Because on the wall—a plain, flat object—is projected a series of images that look and sound like real life. We get so caught up in the experience that we forget where we are, think of the images as being real, and experience feelings about them.

Imagine wearing a white shirt in front of a movie projector, looking at what's being projected onto your shirt, believing that the projection is you, and having feelings about what you see. That's what the unreasonable person's projections are designed to accomplish. Unable or unwilling to tolerate personal wrongness, he projects his negatives onto us so that we become the possessor of them. He accuses us of the very things that are true of him. When we look at what's being projected, believe that the negatives are true of us, and experience emotions about them, we'll think, *Is it me or is it him? It must be me.* At that point the lies have accomplished their confusing purpose.

Finally, drama participation *wears us out*. Dealing with unreasonable people can be absolutely exhausting. They suck the life out of us. They can keep us awake at night. Remember, they are fighting to safeguard a survival-level need—rightness—and they accomplish this through staging dramas. It takes a lot of energy to avoid being enticed into drama participation and to handle it well when it does happen. If it feels like a battle, it is. One client put it this way, "When I'm with him, I experience what happens to Superman when he's around Kryptonite. I lose all my strength."

Three Levels of Unreasonable People

We've been looking at common denominators, but it's important to remember that not all unreasonable people are the same. There are many types and variations, and they exhibit their deficiencies in different ways. They are complex people and have been researched, dissected, and scrutinized from many different angles. Our focus in this book is not so much to analyze them but to understand conflict with them—how it happens and what to do about it. Psychologist Gregory Lester has suggested three levels or degrees of severity.[12] These levels represent degrees of "reason muscle" atrophy.

Dormant (Level 1)

These people are weak in the five "reason muscle" areas and, left to themselves, the muscles remain unused. But an interesting thing occurs when the person being enticed refuses to participate. If the resulting tension is high enough, the Level 1 unreasonable person displays a surprising capacity to grow. The conflict resulting from drama refusal, it seems, may have a growth-producing effect. For Level 1s, conflict is like a relational defibrillator, which shocks the five muscles out of dormancy and into life. He may, for instance, demonstrate surprising remorse for hurting our feelings (empathy). Or he may later explain what a jerk he's been, promise to change, and make actual changes (awareness, responsibility, and reliability). In response to this conflict, he uses reason muscles that had previously seemed nonexistent. For that reason, we use the word *dormant*. The dormant unreasonable person is a jerk who possesses the underlying capability to grow past his jerkhood. When he "hits bottom," he experiences a wake-up call, which serves as a catalyst for change.

Determined (Level 2)

While the Level 1 person may grow in response to drama refusal, the Level 2 unreasonable person becomes more *determined* if he is unable to entice participation. He digs in his heels and stiffens his resolve to win. He can't be wrong and clings to rightness as if his survival depends upon it. He'll claim to be right regardless of all the evidence to the contrary. The determined unreasonable person is a jerk who's convinced himself that you're the jerk. Sadly, conflicts have no growth-producing effects on this person. If he hits bottom, he bounces and appears to learn nothing from the experience.

Dangerous (Level 3)

Everything that's true of the Level 2 is true of the Level 3, with an important addition: *danger.* Physical safety as well as emotional safety is at risk. The prospect of wrongness is so intolerable that he physically injures or even kills his opponent, whom he sees as the enemy. He uses any means necessary to win and feels quite justified in doing so. Examples include domestic abusers, killers who "go postal," terrorists, gang members, mob bosses, and despotic rulers who eliminate, torture, or imprison those with opposing viewpoints. The Level 3 unreasonable person is a dangerous jerk who will hurt or kill. If he hits bottom, he bounces, learns nothing, and comes back up to take us with him to the bottom.

Assessing Unreasonable People

In his book *Washington Goes to War,*[13] the late David Brinkley describes the transformation of Washington, D.C., from a sleepy Southern town into the center of world power. Prior to World War II, he tells us, anyone could tour any public building in Washington at any time because they were just that—buildings that were owned by and, therefore, open to the public. Unescorted citizens could leisurely stroll through the Capitol Building or privately tour the Oval Office when it wasn't in use. The war changed all that. The safety and openness that once characterized our nation's capital were replaced by real dangers and the need for protection from our enemies. Increased threats and actual attacks necessitated security measures that were unimaginable in the 1930s.

Unlike reasonable people, unreasonable people aren't safe. Rather than seeking mutually satisfying conflict solutions, they seek only to win. Consequently, a different set of conflict principles must be used if safety and security are to be maintained. Coaches study game films to understand the opposing team's strengths and weaknesses. Wise generals study the enemy's assets and liabilities before sending troops into battle. For conflict with an unreasonable person to have a good outcome, we must assess the person's "reason muscles," the drama, and the level. We'll use these criteria to assess Patti's mom.

But first, a word of caution. We should form conclusions tentatively and hold conclusions loosely. I knew a lady once who read a book suggesting that all people belong to one of four personality groups. She then routinely referred to individuals by category: "Oh well, what do you expect from Joe. He's a _____. Brenda, on the other hand, is a _____. No wonder they clash." Her discomfort with complexity led to errors of oversimplification, and her labeling people caused her to often misunderstand them. Labels can be helpful but are woefully inadequate when it comes to explaining the intricacies of human behavior. That danger exists in labeling unreasonable people as well.

Remember, people in react mode are at their worst. Since all of us look and sound unreasonable when reacting, we should avoid rushing to judgment. Just as we can't legitimately critique a movie after watching one scene, we should avoid quickly categorizing someone as unreasonable unless we've observed a *pervasive pattern* of behavior over time. "Are we observing transitory unreasonable behavior or is this a persistent pattern of unreasonableness?" is the question we should ask ourselves. Once conclusions are formed, we should be willing to alter them should subsequent evidence suggest otherwise. Additional pattern observations in different settings may result in pleasant surprises or disappointments. Sometimes an unreasonable person turns out to be a reasonable person after all...or the other way around.

Most often, Patti's mom was unreasonable like a Bette Davis vixen. At other times, she was the essence of sweetness, normality, and even reasonableness, like Betty Crocker. This good/bad discrepancy was confusing to Patti and made it difficult to place her mom neatly into a category. Furthermore, Patti didn't like the idea of sticking her mom into the "unreasonable person" box. She desperately wished for a mom who was normal. She found it very painful to admit that her mom's unreasonableness was more than just occasional quirky behavior. It was a persistent pattern that was having a consistently destructive effect.

Patti had tried repeatedly and unsuccessfully to relate to Mom using reasonable person rules, but she finally conceded that a rule shift was now in order.

Assessing the Muscles

When we're in conflict with an unreasonable person, his weak and atrophied reason muscles become apparent. If there were such a thing as a "jerk alert," what would set it off? What follows are ten common weaknesses in each of the five muscle areas.

Humility Muscle Weakness

- He refuses to admit wrongness even when proven wrong.

- He doesn't listen to or consider contrary opinions from anyone.

- He holds his positions rigidly.

- He's "often wrong but never in doubt."

- He audaciously lies, rearranges information, alters history, and appears to sincerely believe his own revisions.

- He skillfully persuades others to believe the revisions.

- He rarely, if ever, apologizes. And if he does, the apology is qualified ("I'm sorry, but you..." or "I've told you I was wrong. Can we now move on?").

- He consistently emphasizes your mistakes and errors.

- He wrongly ascribes to you dishonorable intentions and then attacks you for having them.

- He distorts the meaning of your words and won't allow you to correct the misinterpretation. He hears what he wants to hear.

Awareness Muscle Weakness

- She points out your part of the conflict problem but demonstrates little awareness of her own.

- She's unaware of her negatives that are observable by you and others.
- She defensively resists and makes no use of the feedback given to her by you or others.
- She relishes being the center of attention.
- She's convinced that she's the normal one.
- She denies having certain emotions, such as anger, while clearly displaying them.
- She shifts the focus to you if one of her negatives is exposed ("OK, what about the things you do?").
- She demonstrates little concern about the negative consequences of her words and actions.
- She demonstrates little awareness of your buttons, her reactions, or of how she pushes your buttons.
- She may seem insightful to people who don't know her well.

Responsibility Muscle Weakness

- He refuses to accept blame or to acknowledge fault for anything.
- He is adept at shifting blame onto you or others.
- He seems unbothered when his maturity gaps are revealed.
- His apologies, if given, seem superficial and/or insincere.
- He displays very little personal guilt but often lays guilt trips on you.
- He responds to criticism by saying, "Oh well, that's just the way I am" or "That's just me" or "Hey, I'm not perfect, OK?"
- He frequently accuses you of the very things that characterize him. (The pot calling the kettle black.)
- He skillfully excuses his bad behavior.

- He denies that his bad behavior is bad.
- He projects blame so well that you frequently find yourself wondering, *Is it me or is it him? I don't know, maybe it's me.*

Empathy Muscle Weakness

- She emphasizes her own concerns and gives little attention or value to yours. Conversations are dominated by her interests.
- She attacks not only your position but you personally.
- She knows your buttons and pushes them deliberately when needed.
- She demonstrates little awareness or concern for the toll that her insistence on rightness takes on the relationship. Rightness is more important than relationship.
- Truth or exposed wrongness on her part typically leads to relational alienation or termination.
- She displays discomfort with your feelings or gets mad at you for having them.
- She rarely, if ever, asks you to explain the reasons for your position.
- She doesn't validate your opinions or feelings.
- She seeks first to be understood but rarely seeks to understand.
- She demonstrates the ability to be kind and loving toward you—until you cross her. When this occurs, she turns on you.

Reliability Muscle Weakness

- Insight rarely results in behavior alteration.
- His promises of change can't be trusted. He repents and repeats.

- He says one thing and does another.
- He rarely, if ever, corrects himself.
- He "burns" you by convincing you of his sincerity to change only to repeat the same behaviors.
- He is consistently inconsistent.
- He speaks eloquently of the need to change, but his statements of intent are not followed by actions.
- Change only occurs as a result of forces external to himself.
- He demonstrates little internal motivation to change.
- He sometimes appears to change, but the behavior alteration is short-lived.

While all 50 of these characteristics are not likely to appear in any one person, these are common to unreasonable people. Although all of us display some of them some of the time, for unreasonable people the list represents a consistent pattern.

All five of the "reason muscles" were weak in Patti's mom. *Humility* muscle weakness was evidenced in her starting point assumption: "There's nothing wrong with me, but there's definitely something wrong with you." She lied to herself so routinely that she came to believe her own fabrications and, worse yet, she could snooker others into believing the spin. Some of her friends and neighbors thought, *It's such a shame that this poor nice woman is treated so badly by her neglectful daughter.*

Her *awareness* muscle didn't work. She could clearly see her positives—the same ones Patti appreciated—but was clueless about her negatives. No matter what Patti did or said, her mom couldn't or wouldn't see the problems with herself that Patti was trying to point out.

Her *responsibility* muscle was atrophied from disuse. If her mom was ever caught red-handed in a lie, she'd say, "Oh, so I suppose you've never made a mistake, Little Miss Perfect." Patti was usually stumped by such a remark, being all too familiar with her own imperfections.

Her mom was *empathy* deficient. She demonstrated little, if any, awareness of the impact she was having on Patti's family life. And if she was aware of it, she didn't care. No wonder Patti would often say, "It's all about Mom. She thinks the world is supposed to revolve around her."

Patti's mom's *reliability* muscle didn't work. On occasion Mom would seemingly catch a glimpse of herself and voice what sounded like a change commitment. For instance she might say, "I'm sure I drive you guys crazy sometimes. I need to do a better job of taking care of my own things." But Patti learned to place no stock whatsoever in such statements because they were never followed with actual changes. That's not being pessimistic, just realistic.

Assessing the Drama

Remember, the unreasonable person lacks the "reason muscles" needed to work out a mutually satisfying conflict solution. Consequently, he seeks a different outcome—being right—and the method of reaching that goal is to stage a drama in which he plays the role of good guy. The drama accomplishes its purpose only when he succeeds in getting us to play our required parts so that he can act out his good-guy role.

We can accurately assess his role by paying attention to what's being required of us in the drama. If *subservience* is being required, he is likely playing the role of *master.* His good-guy role is the one who has to take charge of things because no one else can capably do so.

If *gratefulness* is being required, he is likely playing the role of *messiah.* His good-guy role is the one who sacrifices to help people, for which we should be eternally grateful.

If we feel pressured to take care of or *rescue* the person, it is likely that she is playing the role of *martyr.* Her good-guy role is the person who has been unfairly victimized by others, and it is our responsibility to see that she makes it.

If *pretending* is being required, he is likely playing the role of *mute.* His good-guy role is that of an untroubled person who has to contend with someone who insists on stirring up trouble.

Yes, there are times in healthy relationships when we may choose to be submissive, grateful, helpful, or purposely avoidant for the time being. But in unreasonable person dramas, these actions are not voluntary but obligatory, and pressure is exerted until we assume the required position.

Unreasonable people are often referred to as being *manipulative*. If I'm an unreasonable person, my relationship with you can only succeed when you forfeit who you are to become the person I need you to be. If I'm a *master*, I must manipulate you into submission. If I'm a *messiah*, I must manipulate you into becoming a grateful recipient. If I'm a *martyr*, I must manipulate you into becoming a rescuer or a persecutor. If I'm a *mute*, I must manipulate you into pretending that everything is fine. You exist for the purpose of helping me be who I am. I'll stay connected to you only if you play your part. Life is not about you; it's about me.

Patti always called her mom a drama queen, never realizing just how appropriate it was. Without question, her mom's good-guy role was that of a *martyr*, one who struggles in life due to the victimization of others. A victim needs a rescuer and, when the casting call went out, Patti won the part. The unspoken yet very real message from Mom to Patti was, "I can't make it without you, and it'll be your fault if I don't. Live with that." The other subliminal communication was, "We'll have a good, loving relationship as long as you perform your role. If you don't, you'll be sorry." Again, these words were never directly uttered, but the message was as clear as if screamed through a bullhorn.

Mom's preference for the martyr role was understandable considering that she had been victimized by abusive alcoholics. Presumably, at various points along the developmental path, she made choices that solidified her victim stance. As long as Patti could remember, Mom had leaned on her—a role reversal in which the daughter was required to mother the mother. So the current situation was merely a continuation of what had always been. Little wonder, therefore, that Patti felt like she had three children. She did.

The momma dramas unfolded in predictable ways. Sometimes

Mom set up situations in which Patti was required to rescue. For instance, Patti would receive a call from Mom late at night saying that she needed medicine from the drugstore. She was "too sick" to drive and, if she didn't have it, she'd get even sicker, which would be Patti's fault. If Patti bit the bait and made the drugstore run, the drama worked—Mom was the rescued victim. At other times, the audacious intrusion would agitate Patti so much that she'd angrily tell Mom to drive herself to the drugstore. Again, the drama worked—Mom was now the persecuted victim. Either way, when the curtain fell, Mom could take a bow for her brilliant martyr performance.

Patti always wondered if her mom knew what she was doing, if she staged dramas on purpose. I told her it was unlikely that her mom got up every morning and scripted out her performances on a yellow legal pad. It was more likely that drama had become such a deeply entrenched way of relating that she did it without thinking about it. Patti tried occasionally to "call Mom's bluff," explaining to her how she was playing a victim and expecting people to rescue her. It didn't work. If Mom was unaware of it, she would deny the accusation. And if she was aware of it, she certainly wasn't going to admit it. Consequently, direct confrontations did no good.

Assess the Effects

When drama participation *makes us sick,* we say things such as "This makes me want to throw up," "That guy makes my skin crawl," "I need to go take a shower," or "She gives me the creeps." If it *drives us crazy,* we'll say, "Things about him just don't add up," "I feel like I'm in the *Twilight Zone,*" "Is it me or is it him? Maybe it's me," or think, *Who are you, anyway?* When drama *wears us out,* we'll say things such as "I can't ever relax and be myself around him," "I relax so much more when she's not around," "It takes all my energy to deal with him," "I keep playing my conversations with him over and over in my head," or think, *Maybe she'll move.*

Patti always felt manipulated into becoming a rescuer for poor victimized Mom. This manipulation was a violation of her most basic boundary—her sense of self—and the violation set off alarm signals, feelings that occur when a boundary gets crossed. Patti felt used, confused, violated, incensed, presumed upon, taken for granted, hopeless, worn out, and guilty for feeling everything on this list. She felt angry that there was no freedom to just be herself around Mom. Patti even wondered at times just how long Mom would live, and then she felt terrible for thinking such awful thoughts about her own mother.

Assess the Level

Remember the three levels of unreasonable people? Dormant (Level 1), Determined (Level 2), and Dangerous (Level 3). These levels represent degrees of "reason muscle" atrophy. We determine the level by observing the unreasonable person's response to conflict. A Level 1 displays surprising reasonable person characteristics— the opposites of the 50 previously listed. A Level 2 responds to the pressures of conflict by digging in his heels and becoming a worse version of himself. The greater the conflict, the more self-righteously entrenched he becomes inside his defensive fortifications. He will "cut off his nose to spite his face." A Level 3 responds to conflict by threatening us, either overtly or covertly. Life and/or physical well being become jeopardized.

Patti knew her mom wasn't a Level 3 unreasonable person, someone who would hire a hit man to knock her off if she didn't take her to the doctor's office. But she did vacillate between Level 1 and Level 2, wondering which descriptor best fit her mom. At times there were twitches in her seemingly paralyzed "reason muscles," suggesting that she was perhaps a Level 1. But more often than not, she demonstrated no ability whatsoever to tolerate personal wrongness, leading Patti time and again to the Level 2 conclusion. She really wanted her mom to be a Level 1, someone who had the capacity to grow in response to conflict pressure. But Mom repeatedly acted like a Level 2. She reacted to conflict by clinging ever more tenaciously to her need to be right.

The first principle of dealing with the unreasonable is to accurately assess the opposition. The next principle is to avoid participating in unreasonable person dramas.

■ In a Nutshell ■

We can't escape unreasonable people because they are everywhere. They are grown-ups who have under-developed abilities to handle conflict in reasonable ways. The goal of conflict for unreasonable people is not to solve problems but to be right. They accomplish this through staging three-act dramas, which provide opportunities to perform one of several good-guy roles. Drama participation affects us three ways: It makes us sick, drives us crazy, or wears us out.

■ For Reflection ■

1. Are there unreasonable people in your life? What problems have you noticed when trying to resolve differences?

2. Why are unreasonable people willing to sacrifice the truth?

3. Have you found yourself in the midst of an unreasonable person's drama? How did you feel? What did you do?

4. Have you assumed someone was reasonable only to discover he was actually unreasonable? Why do you think it took so long for his unreasonableness to become evident?

5. How would you describe the difference between an "unreasonable person" and a "reasonable person with unreasonable traits"?

Chapter 7

AVOIDING THE DRAMA

I've discovered a way to stay friends forever—
There's really nothing to it.
I simply tell you what to do and you do it.
SHEL SILVERSTEIN

Don't respond to the stupidity of a fool;
you'll only look foolish yourself.
PROVERBS 26:4

Before we had children, Penny and I were talking with a wise couple about the familiar scene of kids throwing grocery store temper tantrums. They explained how they handled this situation with their own children, and we logged their idea for future reference, determined to employ the strategy should we ever need it. A few years later, Penny was in the checkout line and our little girl began begging relentlessly for a piece of junk on a rack nearby. Penny leaned over and said, "Begging is not allowed, and if you ask for it one more time, we'll go home." As expected, she begged again. Penny quietly picked her up, left the cart, and walked out of the store with our girl screaming her head off, conveying to shoppers that a kidnapping was in progress. Penny calmly strapped her into the car seat, drove home, and no other discipline followed. On the next grocery store trip, the begging started again. But this time Penny leaned over and said, "Now, I've told you that begging is not allowed. Remember what happened the last time?" That did it. No more begging. Displeasure, yes; begging, no.

179

What we see is a drama staged and a drama avoided. Our little girl staged the drama hoping to play the role of *master,* to be in charge. But remember, dramas only succeed if others play their parts. Penny avoided participation by neither giving in nor displaying aggravation—two different forms of participating. Therefore, the drama strategy failed and was not attempted the next time around. As good drama critics, let's review this play and make some post-drama observations.

- To handle this situation so well, Penny had to go against her grain. She was prone to get pulled into the power struggle, get upset, argue, threaten, or (worse yet) give in to keep the peace. She countered her natural reactions by opting, instead, for preplanned responses. *Drama avoidance requires planning.*

- The strategy cost her something—she had to go back to the store and shop again. But we had previously determined that the cost of reinforcing this undesirable pattern was higher than the time and energy it cost her to reshop. *Drama avoidance may cost something.*

- In this case, our plan succeeded on the first attempt, but Penny was prepared to repeat the strategy if needed until it did work. *Drama avoidance requires persistence.*

- The outcome of our plan had a good effect, in this case for both parties. Penny got to shop with less aggravation. Our girl was forced to grow up just a little bit that day, developing better ways of handling herself. *Drama avoidance brings about growth.*

Again, unreasonable people are children in the bodies of adults. They stage dramas not unlike the one just discussed, which succeed only if others participate. Participation provides a stage on which the unreasonable person's drama is performed. How can we avoid becoming drama participants? By avoiding three enticements: button pushes, reactions, and pushing buttons.

Avoiding Button Pushes

Unreasonable People Know Our Buttons

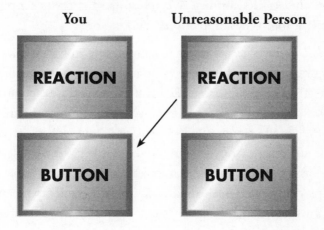

The unreasonable person pushes our buttons hoping for a reaction. He typically understands us better than we understand him. He or she knows where our buttons are and how to push them. Unreasonable people are good at enticing participation because drama success is perceived as necessary for their survival. Reasonable people are not naturally good at resisting enticements because that's not how we relate. Therefore, we must develop the skill.

Expect Attacks

The unreasonable person may push our buttons in predictably obvious ways or ambush us in unpredictably subtle ways.

Obvious Attacks

Examples of obvious attacks include insults, besmirching of character, slanderous accusations, name-calling, defamations, unjustified criticisms, and blatant lies. The unreasonable person taunts and eggs us on, hoping desperately for a knee-jerk reaction that places us squarely into the drama.

Subtle Attacks (Manipulations)

While obvious attacks are actively aggressive, subtle attacks are passively aggressive or manipulative. Our buttons get pushed, but we don't see the attacks coming. We get ambushed or sucker-punched. Let's look at four types of manipulations.

Exploitation of weaknesses. An invading army attacks at the weakest spot. Terrorists strike where their opponents are most vulnerable. Similarly, the unreasonable person sniffs out our weaknesses and attacks us there. We all have buttons—places of weakness, immaturity, and inadequacy. When life requires us to be strong in a weak area, an internal dialogue takes place. Some people use the word "tapes" to describe this self-talk, as in "When I took that job, all of my old inadequacy tapes started playing, telling me I couldn't do it." Others refer to the dialogue using terms such as "the voices," "the committee," or "the choir." One British writer described it using a phrase from wartime England: "the internal saboteur."[1] The unreasonable person, who wants to defeat us in conflict, studies our weaknesses and allies himself with our internal saboteurs. When certain buttons are pushed, the internal saboteurs spring into action, doing their best to remind us of our weakness and make us feel awful about ourselves. Like a voice-activated recorder, the sound of his voice on the outside activates the tapes on the inside. If we believe the tapes, we get sucked into the drama and the exploitation succeeds.

Suppose you are generous to a fault. You're a very giving person, but an old tape inside your head says, *You really could do more for people, you know. What's wrong with you? You're so selfish.* Suppose also that you have someone in your life like Patti's mom, a Level 2 martyr, whose stance is, "I can't make it without you to rescue me." She constantly demands assistance for problems she could easily fix herself. If you decline a request, she says, "That's fine. I'll do it myself. I thought you were here for me, but I guess I was wrong." Your internal saboteur springs into action saying, *She's right, you know. If you were a better person, you'd go out of your way to help her. What's wrong with you?* You've been guilt tripped, and to escape the guilt, you acquiesce to the demand. Your weakness has been exploited, and you've become a player in the drama, saving a martyr supposedly in need of rescue.

Projections. In Chapter 6, we talked about projections. Unable to tolerate personal wrongness, the unreasonable person takes his negatives and projects them on us so that we become the possessor of them. When successful, he accuses us of the very things that are true of him, and we believe the accusations. We think, *Is it me or is it him? It must be me.*

Presumptions. Most of us have been taught to believe the best of people and to give them the benefit of the doubt. While reasonable people deserve such courtesies, unreasonable people don't. As a kind gesture, we may offer a ride to a hitchhiker. If he's a good guy, no problem. If he's a crook, our kindness gets us robbed. If we give an unreasonable person the benefit of the doubt, he may very well presume upon our good graces and use it to his advantage—a subtle attack.

Role shifts. If an unreasonable person can't entice us into playing the required part, he may shift roles in hopes that, when the drama ends, he'll be back in his preferred role.[2] Here are some different forms of role shifting:

If the *master role* is preferred: A master needs us to submit. If we don't, he may shift into the *messiah role,* someone rescuing a person in need. He gives us something, but the gift has strings attached. At that point the giver is no longer a helper but a controller, the assistance being accompanied by an obligation to submit.

If the *messiah role* is preferred: A messiah is a sacrificial giver and needs us to be grateful recipients. If we aren't, she may slip into the *martyr role,* saying, "After all I've done for you, this is the kind of treatment I get? Thanks a lot." If it works, we'll allow her to resume the messiah role so we can escape the guilt trip discomfort.

If the *martyr role* is preferred: Martyrs are either saved by messiahs or persecuted by masters, the roles we must play for the martyr role to succeed. If we don't, she may become a *master* and strike at us, hoping we'll strike back. If we do strike back, she can once again assume the role of a martyr, a person who suffers at the hands of others: "I can't believe you would treat me this way."

If the *mute role* is preferred: A mute wants to be untroubled and needs us to pretend along with him that everything is just fine. If we refuse to participate in the pretense or enable the denial, he may assume the role of a *martyr:* "We could get on with our lives if you wouldn't keep bringing up all our problems. Can we please move on?"

These role requirements are button-pushing, boundary-violating drama enticements. There is pressure to perform our roles so that the other's role achieves the desired outcome—becoming the good guy. That's why it wears us out. We can't relax and just be ourselves.

Learn from Your Mistakes

Pickpockets can do their chosen profession because people aren't expecting their pockets to get picked. Remember, unreasonable people are good at enticements, but reasonable people are not naturally good at resisting enticements and can easily get caught off guard. We will make mistakes, and slip-ups are inevitable. But it's important to learn from our mistakes and avoid repeating them. As the saying goes, "Burn me once, shame on you. Burn me twice, shame on me." Beating ourselves up about slip-ups doesn't help, but safeguarding ourselves against further enticements does. We should avoid situations in which mistakes are likely to happen and rehearse how to handle the situation should it happen again.

When Patti Avoided Button Pushes

Long before she came to see me, Patti used the term "subtly manipulative" to describe her mom. To casual observers, she was always the pleasant and productive Betty Crocker, but to Patti and Bill she was frequently a Bette Davis-type vixen. Patti learned she had to keep up her guard in this game of "emotional chess" between her family and "the vixen."

Patti's mom was quite adept at utilizing her arsenal of subtle weapons. Her daughter had a tender spot for people and animals in need and would go out of her way to provide assistance whenever she could. Understanding this, her mom would make her own needs apparent, taking on the demeanor of a wounded pet. These attempts to capitalize on Patti's bigheartedness usually worked. When they did, Patti felt angry and presumed upon one more time. Yes, her mom was manipulative, but Patti came to see that it was her responsibility to avoid manipulation. When she studied her own buttons and worked out a better response, it became much harder for her mom to push them.

Having to think this way about her mom left Patti with a bad taste in her mouth, reflected in statements such as, "I can't believe I have to be so guarded with my own mother. Isn't that terrible?" Actually, Patti wasn't being terrible, she was being wise. The guilt she felt for having negative feelings about her mom was unwarranted. Her bad feelings served a good purpose—to make her aware of boundary violations. She couldn't feel good about what her mother was doing, but she could make use of what she felt to move toward good conflict.

Avoid Reactions

Controlling your reaction when your button is pushed

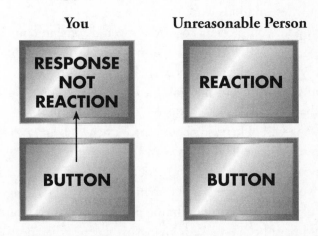

Rudyard Kipling must have known some cantankerous unreasonable people. He said, "If you can keep your head when all about you are losing theirs and blaming it on you..."[3] The unreasonable person desperately needs us to react, to lose our heads, so our reactions can be used as evidence that we're crazy and he or she is not.

Figuratively speaking, he takes "snapshots" of our reactions and uses those images to build the case—to himself and others—that we're bad and he's good. "Photo albums" displaying pictures of our bad behavior are eagerly shown around. Another way to think about this is that he has an emotional "remote control" for us. When he pushes our buttons and observes a reaction, he's gratified. But if he doesn't see a reaction, he's frustrated and will push the buttons more vigorously. To keep from reacting, we must plan our responses so we won't display any reaction, thus stopping the manipulation.

Plan Your Response

A friend of mine had a business partner who was a world-class jerk—a Level 2 *master*. Frequently his partner would storm into my friend's office and ream him out for some inconsequential reason. My friend would wait for a pause and say, "That's all very interesting. Got any plans for the weekend?" The partner would spew for a few seconds and leave the office muttering, "You're impossible." My friend would then calmly return to his work.

Hearing the commotion, co-workers would come into my friend's office and say, "Why do you let him walk all over you like that? If I were you, I'd get in his face, shake my finger, call him a few names, and tell him I'm not going to take it anymore. Why don't you do that?" My friend, it turns out, was not being a weenie. No, he was being wise. He wasn't being "nice"; he was being *nonreactive*. Through experience he'd discovered that angry reactions were just what his partner wanted. Sure, my friend wanted to strike back. But to do so would have played right into his partner's hands. Angry reactions would have made him a drama participant, and the rest of his day would have been wrecked, giving his partner the control he so desperately wanted. And the resulting lack of productivity would have been blamed on him.

Reactions are impulsive; *responses are intentional.* The drama enticement with my friend failed because he had a preplanned, rehearsed way to respond. He thwarted the drama by refusing to be intimidated by his partner's obnoxious rants. Had he not planned this response, he would have impulsively reacted, placing him squarely into the drama.

To plan responses, we need to know what role is being required of us. If our unreasonable person is a *master,* we'll need to plan ways to avoid subservience, like my friend did in the example. If the person is a *messiah,* we'll need to avoid the obligatory role of gratitude. If he is a *martyr,* we'll need to find ways to avoid being guilted into rescuing behaviors like Patti had to do. If he is a *mute,* we'll need to avoid participating in the pretence that all is well.

It's usually best to refuse our roles quietly rather than confrontationally. Had my friend said, "I know what you're up to, and I'm not going to allow you to dominate this office with your anger," that statement alone would have made him a drama participant. Instead, he refused quietly, disallowing his partner the gratification of observing a reaction.

If we don't react, the unreasonable person will likely think his emotional remote control is broken and try to fix it by pushing the buttons harder. In the short term, he may become a worse version of himself. If we don't remember this, we might think, "This isn't helping; it's hurting." Actually, more vigorous button pushing on the unreasonable person's part shows that our plan is succeeding!

Display No Reaction

In the early 1960s, college students from Northern states volunteered to help with Southern voter registration drives, especially encouraging African-Americans to exercise their right to vote. It was dangerous work and, as history has recorded, some lost their lives. Understanding the way the system worked in the South at that time, the organizers fully expected many of the volunteers to be arrested.

They knew that bigoted law enforcement officials would provoke the civil rights activists, hoping to elicit violent reactions that would provide justifiable grounds for arrest.

So prior to heading south, the leaders created simulations in which some students played the parts of civil rights workers and others played the parts of law enforcement officials. The "officials" would scream racial epithets, kick at them, and insult them. In response to these ugly provocations, the volunteers were trained to say and do nothing. They were to lie down on the ground and go limp, staving off every natural impulse to strike back. By doing so they would deprive the provokers of legitimate reasons to arrest them. They would still be arrested, but on trumped up charges that could be challenged and overturned in the courts. This strategy of nonviolent resistance, also used by Mahatma Gandhi and Martin Luther King, was extremely powerful in bringing change to institutional structures that had been dominated by controlling, unreasonable people for a long time.

On a smaller scale, that's exactly what we need to do with unreasonable people who push our buttons, hoping desperately for a reaction that can be used against us. It's not that we won't have reactions, but that we *choose not to display them.* We need to restrain externally what we feel internally. This idea has been expressed through adages such as "Never let 'em see you sweat," "The best response is no response," and "Don't feed into it." Card players learn to wear "poker faces" for this very reason. The adage "Kill 'em with kindness" applies here because displaying kindness versus agitation disallows the drama enticement. Displaying no reaction keeps us out of the drama. *And that's not being passive; it's being powerful.*

When Patti Avoided Reactions

No one could get under Patti's skin like her mother. Whenever she did, Patti was most prone to react, either by fulfilling her rescuing role or by getting angry. Either way, the drama worked to reestablish her mom in the starring role of *martyr.* So Patti had to work on both types of reactions. First she had to preplan ways to resist her mom's rescuing enticements so she wouldn't get caught off guard.

- She rehearsed several ways to verbalize a *polite decline.* That is, she would respectfully say no when unreasonable requests were made.

- She stopped explaining her reasons. Previously she felt obligated to explain why a request was being declined. The problem was that her mom always found ways to invalidate her reasons, leaving her with no excuse. Patti's explanations became more generic: "It's not going to work for us to do that tonight." If Mom asked why not, Patti would say something else generic: "Oh, a bunch of different things. I better run. We'll talk to you later in the week."

- She reminded herself that declining requests would make things seem worse in the short run, understanding that Mom would locate her guilt button and push it vigorously. But like my wife and daughter in the grocery store, Patti knew the long-term payoff was worth the short-term cost.

Patti also had to fight against unwarranted guilt. With her head, she saw the necessity of staying out of the momma drama, understanding the toll it was taking on her, her marriage, and her kids. With her feelings, however, she felt guilty of being heartlessly cruel to a person in need. She had to remind herself that rescuing Mom wasn't helping her but enabling her to perpetuate some long-standing dysfunctional patterns.

Second, Patti had to keep from displaying externally the emotions she felt internally, the chief of which was anger. The pattern of Patti's reactions to Mom's rescuing enticements was this: give in, give in, give in, blowup, give in, give in, give in, blowup. But when the blowups occurred, Mom would always say, "I've never understood why you get so mad. But then you've always had a really short fuse. I just wish you wouldn't take it out on me. Is everything OK with you and Bill?" In this way, Mom had mastered the art of using Patti's anger to reinforce her victim stance: "I'm an innocent person being raged at by an angry person." Since open displays of anger were used against her, Patti practiced these responses:

- Say nothing in response to Mom's provocations. Most often Patti found that the best response was no response. When Mom attempted long and wordy guilt trips, Patti learned to say, "Uh huh."

- Use matter-of-fact delivery rather than an angry tone. Patti's every impulse was to "let her mom have it," but she knew if she did her mom would make Patti's anger the focus rather than addressing the issue at hand.

- Politely excuse herself from conversations. Patti often found that the longer they talked, the more likely she was to cave, to give in to the enticement to rescue. Leaving the conversation wasn't being avoidant; it was being wise.

Avoid Pushing Buttons

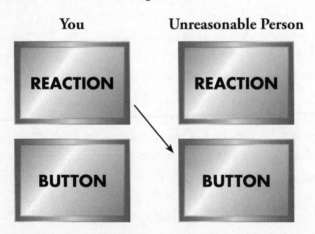

Controlling Your Actions

The third way to resist the drama is to avoid pushing the unreasonable person's buttons. If we follow our natural inclinations and react by pushing those buttons, we're in the drama. For instance, an exasperated reasonable person will sometimes exclaim to an unreasonable person, "You need counseling." That pushes the unreasonable person's buttons because what he hears is, "There's something wrong with you." He won't make use of that suggestion because he has no "reason muscles," so he resorts to drama as a way to deal with the conflict. If it works, he winds up as the good guy and you as the bad guy. The idea of not pushing buttons is expressed through these statements:

- Leave well enough alone.
- Let sleeping dogs lie.
- Don't stir the pot.
- Don't poke a hornet's nest.

There are two common thoughts that occur to reasonable people arguing with unreasonable people. One is, *How can he possibly believe that nonsense? If I could just get him to understand the sensibleness of my position, we could resolve this problem.* Here we're attempting to establish reason. But remember, the person we're dealing with is not interested in reason, only in rightness.

The other common thought is, *I'll teach him a lesson and make him see the error of his ways.* Now we're attempting to establish justice. But the unreasonable person won't see those errors because he admits no wrongness. Expecting either reason or justice "pokes the hornet's nest" and keeps us caught in the drama.

Don't Expect Reasonableness

Let's go back to the grocery store drama at the beginning of this chapter. Suppose Penny had said this when our child threw her tantrum:

> I need you to understand my position here. I'm not buying that junk on the rack because it's expensive and bad for you. Now, does it make sense for you to keep begging for it? No. All righty then, we've got that straight.

With 100-percent certainty that wouldn't have worked. Why? Because it would have been attempting to reason with someone who was being unreasonable. And the exasperation displayed would have made Penny a drama participant.

The common temptation when arguing with an unreasonable person is to make our case more vigorously, hoping that he'll eventually get it. What we discover, however, is that no matter what we say or how well we say it, the person won't get it. He'll not listen to, understand, or validate our position. If we react by arguing harder, we're right back in the drama. We lose simply by becoming engaged in the conversational tug of war.

So remember this rule of thumb: *To solve conflict problems with reasonable people, we should talk more. To solve conflict problems with unreasonable people, we should talk less and act more* (see Chapter 8 for more details). Conversations with reasonable people can accomplish something, but conversations with unreasonable people accomplish nothing. We can't reason with an unreasonable person. They "win" by keeping us frustratingly embroiled in the verbal battle.

In the grocery store scenario, Penny addressed the temper tantrum problem not with words but with actions—calmly picking our child up and leaving the store. Had she engaged in a verbal power struggle, she would have lost, and the drama would have accomplished its purpose—establishing our little girl as the controlling good guy with a frustrated, out-of-control parent.

Don't Expect Justice

One of my favorite shows growing up was *Perry Mason*. Each episode followed the same formula. An innocent person would be accused of murder. Perry Mason would be hired as the defense attorney and win the case, out-dueling the prosecuting attorney, Mr. Burger. The climactic moment of each episode came when Perry would reveal the actual killer, who was usually being grilled on the witness stand by Perry at the time. Having been exposed, the guilty person would tearfully and candidly confess, to the chagrin of Mr. Burger, who would then move for all charges against the defendant to be dropped. Despite its predictability, Perry Mason was a "feel good" show because, each week, a Level 3 (dangerous) unreasonable person was brought to justice. Not only that, the killer would openly confess, telling exactly how and why the murder was committed.

Seeing a bad guy get caught and taking responsibility for his crime feels good, and we love to see that happen in real life. Unfortunately, such open admissions of guilt on the part of unreasonable people are rare. Most often, guilty unreasonable people cling to their innocence despite mounds of evidence to the contrary. They may experience consequences, but their unwillingness to vocalize responsibility leaves us with an incomplete sense of justice—and that feels bad.

Any attempt by us to establish justice will put us into the thick of the drama. It's very tempting to say, "I'll teach him a lesson so he won't do that anymore." The problem is that unreasonable people learn no lessons because that would require the use of muscles they've allowed to atrophy. We want them to 'fess up just like the killers on *Perry Mason*. But trying to get them to admit wrongness won't work and, if we display frustration, we've become drama participants. We may not be able to achieve observable justice, but we can set boundaries (see Chapter 8 for more on setting boundaries).

In Chapter 6, I referred to the movie *It's a Wonderful Life* to illustrate unreasonable people and their dramas. A number of years ago *Saturday Night Live* had a Christmas skit portraying what they called the "Lost Ending" of that movie. The skit begins where the real movie ends, with the citizens of Bedford Falls celebrating the financial rescue of their beloved friend, George Bailey. Just then it's revealed that Mr. Potter is in possession of the money that George was in trouble for losing. Filled with rage and indignation, the citizens turn into a lynch mob, storm Mr. Potter's house, and beat the stuffing out of him.

This "lost ending" taps into something for which we all long—justice. But with unreasonable people, we often don't get to observe the kind of justice that has a person admitting wrongness and/or suffering consequences. Many unreasonable people "get away with murder" literally or figuratively. Like Mr. Potter, they admit nothing and seemingly experience no adverse consequences for their bad behavior. Trying to establish justice, to force an unreasonable person to acknowledge personal wrongness against his will, has a button-pushing effect and provides a way for him to keep us wrapped up in his drama.

When Patti Avoided Pushing Buttons

For a long time Patti indulged the notion that if she could only get her mom to see what she was doing, she'd stop. Both she and Bill spent a lot of time and energy trying to get Mom to understand that she could, in fact, do more for herself than she was doing. "We want you to be more independent and self-sufficient," they reasoned with her. But everything they said fell on deaf ears. The problem was that Mom preferred victimhood over independence, so none of their logical arguments ever registered. Getting Mom to see their point about self-sufficiency was like "trying to chisel through a stainless steel wall with a plastic spoon," as Patti put it. The more they talked, the more entrenched Mom became, and the more frustrated Patti got. Mom would then make note of Patti's frustration, wondering aloud why her daughter was always so angry. The *martyr* drama was fulfilling its purpose beautifully.

Patti came to see that she and Bill were attempting the impossible—reasoning with an unreasonable person. If Mom had no "reason muscles," logical arguments would never penetrate her tightly constructed defensive barrier. Attempts to reason resulted not in solutions but in frustration, which Mom then used against them. So instead of relying on words, Patti and Bill devoted more energy to setting boundaries. Boundaries accomplished what reasoning never could.

Patti was angry at her mother for all of this and, to be honest, sometimes entertained fantasies of revenge. She felt urges to strike back, hoping Mom would feel some of the pain she felt. But were she to do so, Mom would be more gratified than hurt, happy for a new opportunity to play the wounded martyr. Consequently, Patti and Bill had to let go of the need to exact justice, knowing Mom was unwilling or unable to learn the lessons one is supposed to learn from negative consequences.

Here is a summary of the best ways to respond to an unreasonable person.

Drama Control

Avoid Button Pushes	Avoid Reacting	Avoid Pushing Buttons
Expect attacks Learn from your mistakes	Plan your response Display no reaction	Don't expect reasonableness Don't expect justice

Good conflict with unreasonable people involves assessing our opposition and avoiding the drama. It also involves what's discussed in the next chapter—accepting limits.

In a Nutshell

Unreasonable people don't have the reason muscles required to solve conflict problems, so they opt for a different goal: rightness. They reach this goal by staging dramas, which succeed only with our participation. We can avoid the drama by resisting three enticements: our buttons being pushed, our reactions, and pushing the unreasonable person's buttons.

For Reflection

1. What is the cost of drama avoidance? What is the gain?

2. What four common types of manipulations are used by unreasonable people to entice your participation in their drama?

3. Reactions are automatic; responses are _____.

4. How does displaying no reaction help diffuse a drama?

5. What part does guilt play in unreasonable person relationships? Give some examples.

6. Why is justice not a reasonable expectation when dealing with an unreasonable person?

Chapter 8

ACCEPTING THE LIMITS

*Love your neighbor
but don't pull down your hedge.*
BENJAMIN FRANKLIN

*Keep vigilant watch over your heart;
that's where life starts.*
PROVERBS 4:23

We've been discussing Patti, a person in conflict with an unreasonable person. Here's a similar story, only this conflict was not between individuals but between nations—the United States and the Soviet Union. In 1917, the Bolshevik Revolution occurred. The Russian monarchy was overthrown and replaced by a communist form of government. The new Union of Soviet Socialist Republics was founded upon Marxist principles, bringing radical changes to this vast country that stretched from Europe's border to the Pacific. Though allied against Hitler's Germany in World War II, the United States and the Soviet Union distrusted each other, with suspicions coming to a head in the years following the war. The development of Soviet nuclear capabilities in the late 1940s kept tensions escalated for the next several decades as the planet endured the ever-present potential of thermonuclear annihilation.

We've all struggled to handle conflicts with individual unreasonable people. But in many respects, the United States at this time had to contend with a giant, global unreasonable person in the form of the Soviet Union. This applied not so much to individual citizens but to the communist leadership controlling the apparatus of government. Here's what we'd find if we used Chapter 6's criteria for assessing the opposition.

First, they had unused "reason muscles." Their worldview and ideologically driven commitments led them to believe:

- The wrongness must be on the side of the U.S.
- We only see where we're right.
- If we're wrong, so what?
- We're only bothered if the wrongness of the U.S. hurts us.
- We're not wrong, so there is nothing to correct.

They truly believed they were good and the U.S. was bad. They accused the U.S. of the very things that were true of them. So great was their commitment to rightness that they were willing to sacrifice truth to maintain it. The ends justified the means. They believed that lying or any other vice was a virtue if it advanced the cause of world communism.

Second, they were Level 3 (dangerous) unreasonable people. They responded to conflict by threatening to annihilate the U.S. or anyone who challenged them.

Third, they were *masters* who needed others to play a subservient role. Their "satellites" in Eastern Europe had no independence, and any moves toward self-determination were soundly squelched by military force.

Fourth, Western nations, particularly the United States, experienced the same effects as those produced by individual unreasonable people. The USSR government drove us crazy, made us sick, and wore us out. The situation drained huge portions of our national resources.

Bad conflict is what happens when we react to each other's reactions. Armed with atomic weapons that could be delivered atop intercontinental ballistic missiles (ICBMs), the two nations could ill-afford bad conflict reactions. One of these almost occurred in 1962 when the Soviets attempted to deploy offensive nuclear weapons on the island of Cuba, placing American population centers within striking distance of

Soviet missiles. This was unacceptable to the U.S. and, for a few days, the world teetered on the precipice of nuclear war, in which an attack by either side would have led to retaliation by the other. In this case, the reactive cycle would have resulted in millions of deaths.

To avoid the horrific effects of bad conflict, the two nations became engaged in what was called the "Cold War," a conflict in which few shots were fired but tensions remained escalated. It wasn't a hot, shooting war due largely to the policy of "Mutually Assured Destruction" (MAD). That is, a nuclear first strike by either side would trigger a retaliatory response by the other, assuring the destruction of the initiator. Thus, the policy served to deter first strike impulses. "Peaceful coexistence" was the term used to describe the Cold War relationship of the two superpowers. While MAD helped to lower the potential of bad conflict, there was still the question about how to have good conflict with a giant, global unreasonable person. A vigorous debate developed among Westerners about how peace could best be achieved.

Generally there were two schools of thought. The first was the "peace through reason" approach. This view held that the Soviet leaders were reasonable people and wanted peace just like us; we simply misunderstood each other. The expectation, therefore, was that Western disarmament gestures would impress the Soviets and be reciprocated by their own disarmament gestures, making the world an increasingly safer place. The other school of thought was the "peace through strength" approach. This view held that the Soviet leaders were less interested in peace and more interested in winning, in achieving their global ideological objectives. Consequently, Western disarmament gestures would simply be exploited by the Soviets, giving them a position of nuclear superiority and making the world an even more dangerous place.

For many years the "peace through reason" approach was attempted, and the Soviets did in fact exploit it to gain the upper hand, leaving the prospects for peace even more elusive. Then, in the early 80s, we shifted strategies and began dealing with the Soviets as global Level 3 masters who wanted to win. The "peace through strength" method was employed. The U.S. refused to play its designated role in the unreasonable person drama—subservience. We increased rather than decreased the strength of our military. For the Soviets, the expense of regaining and maintaining the superior position placed an unsustainable burden on their already faltering economy. Thus, military superiority, the master role, became economically impossible for them. This, plus the growing discontent of the masses within Russia and its satellite states, led to the downfall of the Soviet system and the end of the Cold War.

This is a story of good conflict with an unreasonable nation. The Cold War ended not because the U.S. was nice but because the U.S. was strong. It's not that the Soviets became reasonable, but that they became realistic. They changed because internal pressures made holding to their system no longer feasible. We didn't change their minds; we changed the conditions. And when the conditions changed, they changed their minds. Good conflict was achieved because the U.S. did two things: set relational boundaries and acknowledged relational realities.

Setting Relational Boundaries

With reasonable people we solve problems by working together to reach mutually satisfying solutions. Reasoning with reasonable people works, which makes for good conflict. But it doesn't work with unreasonable people because they don't have the necessary "reason muscles." And if we attempt it, the frustration we experience puts us right back into their drama.

Reasoning doesn't work, but a limited substitute does—setting boundaries. Boundaries accomplish what reasoning can't. In Chapter 2 I talked about Mr. Jones, the man who had the obnoxious neighbor with the obnoxious dog that regularly dug up his flowers, scattered his garbage, and fertilized his grass. He tried everything he could to convince the neighbor to leash the mutt but nothing worked. Finally he improved the situation by putting up a fence. In this case, the solution that couldn't be achieved through reasoning was achieved through boundaries. Yes, it cost him something, but it worked. With reasonable people, problems are solved when both sides participate in the reasoning process. With unreasonable people, problems are "restrained" when the reasonable person does a good job of setting boundaries.

A gentle reminder: All aspects of dealing with unreasonable people—assessing them, avoiding their dramas, accepting the limits—are challenging. So challenging, in fact, that we won't succeed without the support of others. Unreasonable people can be so confounding, so determined, and so frustrating that we'll fail if we try to go it alone. The understanding and reinforcement of other reasonable people is not a luxury but a necessity. Slaves in the pre-Civil War South understood this well. For all practical purposes, their masters operated under this unreasonable set of assumptions: "We're good, you're bad, you exist for us. If you submit to our control, we'll get along just fine." Lack of submission led to physical harm. Their sufferings under that system of chattel slavery were eased somewhat by singing songs that came to be known as "Negro Spirituals." Through the lyrics, they expressed thoughts and feelings to each other about their trials, their tribulations, and their hopes. The ability to endure was enhanced through mutual encouragement.

We may not be literally enslaved by unreasonable people, but the need for support is just as essential. Remember, the unreasonable person believes his survival depends upon getting us to believe "There's nothing wrong with him, but there's definitely something wrong with us." Without reference points for our sanity that others provide, it's very easy to get swept into that distortion and become discouraged. *Good conflict with unreasonable people is achievable only with the support of reasonable people relationships.*

Let's look now at principles involved in setting relational boundaries with each of the three levels of unreasonable people.

Setting Boundaries with Level 1 (Dormant) Unreasonable People

Left to himself, the Level 1 unreasonable person doesn't change. But when the person he needs to entice into the drama refuses to cooperate, it creates conflict pressure. And if the pressure is high enough, he displays a surprising capacity to grow, which is why the word *dormant* is used. As stated in Chapter 6, conflict serves as a relational defibrillator that shocks the "reason muscles" into use. Our goal with a Level 1 unreasonable person is to use boundaries that promote *growth*. We can't make growth happen, but we can create conditions under which growth is more likely to occur. The experience of dealing with a Level 1 unreasonable person is very similar to that of being a toddler's parent, an elementary schoolteacher, or a coach. It takes a lot of work, but the outcome is worth the effort. We have to be frustrating, persistent, and patient.

Be Frustrating

By advising you to be frustrating, I don't mean that we are to be maliciously hurtful. I do mean that we should intentionally frustrate the drama process by refusing to play our designated roles so the resulting discomfort gives the unreasonable person an incentive to grow. That's what happened in the grocery store checkout line when Penny refused to participate in the verbal tug of war with our daughter. When it became clear to our little girl that she couldn't get Penny to play her part, she was forced to grow up a little. Refusing roles such as subservience, gratefulness, rescuing, or pretending discombobulates the unreasonable person, making him feel uncomfortable. But that's good because that feeling may cause him or her to seek out more mature ways of relating.

Be Persistent

Atrophied muscles will only become usable through repetitive exercise. When we frustrate the unreasonable person, we are forcing him to use unused muscles that will get stronger only when he uses them repetitively. No one gets in shape after one trip to the gym. The unreasonable person tries repeatedly to entice us into drama participation. We have to repeatedly frustrate that enticement.

Be Patient

Remember, unreasonable people are children in the bodies of adults. Children don't grow up overnight; it takes time. And some unreasonable people take longer to grow than others. Like all of us, they easily slip back into old, familiar patterns. When this happens, we may be tempted to think, *This is too hard. It isn't working.* We must remind ourselves to take the long view.

Be Encouraged to Stay with It

In dealing with a Level 1 unreasonable person, we need the encouragement of others to stay with the process. When we are prone to throw in the towel, we need others who will remind us that what we're doing is worth it. The outcome of good conflict with a Level 1 unreasonable person is helping someone become a better version of himself.

I had a client once whose husband gave every indication of being a Level 2 master. From a distance he was funny, likeable, engaging, bright, and accomplished. But up close everything had to run a particular way—his. He seemed incapable of working through any conflict. He and his wife were drifting further and further apart. His wife suggested counseling, but he refused, saying, "I don't need some weird shrink telling me what to do. I'm not crazy. You go if you want." At this time he met a gorgeous but dim-witted sycophant who lavished upon him the ego strokes he so desperately craved in his idealized world. When my client discovered the affair, the prognosis for her marriage was poor. Immediately following the disclosure, her husband became entrenched in self-justification, using the audacious excuse that his tawdry fling was somehow her fault. Now he was demanding that the subject be dropped and discussed no more so they could "move on with their lives."

But she refused to participate in the cover-up, knowing that if she acquiesced to his demands, their gaping marital wounds would never stop bleeding. Nothing would change if she didn't do something drastically different. So she insisted that he live elsewhere—not as a move toward divorce but as a move toward the possibility of reconciliation. He was frustrated about it, and he didn't like it one bit. But he found another place, and they stayed separated for the next several months.

Then something happened that was totally unanticipated. He told her that the possibility of divorce had hit him like a ton of bricks, and he expressed remorse for his actions. He acknowledged the wrongness of his choices and asked for forgiveness. She told him that forgiveness was possible, but trust would be more difficult to reestablish. Surprisingly, he said he understood and was willing to do whatever was needed to do so. Rightfully so, she was extremely cautious and reluctant to put much stock in his uncharacteristic words of contrition. Though she considered it, she didn't allow him to move back in just yet. She needed time to see if his behaviors lined up with his statements of intent. As time went by, she didn't observe perfection, but she was impressed with the congruency of his words and actions.

Everything didn't go smoothly, but they worked on it. They sought counseling as individuals and as a couple. They had rough times and difficult discussions about what happened (the affair) and why it happened (the relational problems that precipitated the affair). They had arguments in which old, bad conflict patterns emerged. But in these arguments he demonstrated an uncommon willingness to acknowledge personal shortcomings and a sensitivity to her thoughts and feelings. He was open to her input and made use of it. His "reason muscles," which had previously seemed nonexistent, were being used and gradually becoming stronger. She also surrounded herself with close friends who knew about their reconciliation attempts and supported what they were trying to accomplish. After a lengthy period, they mutually decided to live under the same roof. They continued formal counseling for quite some time and didn't stop working on their relationship when that ended. They developed a network of couples through a local church, and each also cultivated close individual friendships. I still hear from them on occasion, and the good conflict patterns they began have continued.

When this wife and I first met, the marital prognosis was grim, and when the husband had the affair, it looked even worse. But her strong response to a bad thing had a good outcome. She couldn't change him, but she could change the conditions. And when the conditions changed, he decided that personal change was necessary and demonstrated a surprising capacity to grow. We thought he was a Level 2, but he turned out to be a Level 1. He grew past his jerkhood and is now a reasonable person. And they are both becoming increasingly better versions of themselves as a result of good conflict.

Setting Boundaries with Level 2 (Determined) Unreasonable People

Level 1s can grow if we refuse drama participation, but Level 2s won't. They just try more vigorously to entice us into their dramas. And if they continue to fail, they may sever the relationship. As one client told me, "You have to relate to my dad on his terms. If you don't, you cease to exist." Our goal with these people is not for them to grow but for us to contain the effects of their dysfunction on our lives. Let's go back to the obnoxious neighbor with the irritating dog. The fence didn't cause the neighbor to grow and become better, but it did make living next to him tolerable. Even if he continues to be his nasty self on his side, the fence keeps the reasonable person from being affected so much by the nuisance dog—unless, of course, the neighbor teaches his dog to fly. Containment makes relationships with Level 2s manageable. We establish boundaries by being expectant, firm, and insulated.

Be Expectant

We should expect unreasonable people to be unreasonable, to display many of the 50 characteristics listed in Chapter 6. They'll say or do something offensive or stiffen their resolve to be right no matter what we say or how we say it. The oft-used phrase that expresses what we have to do is "consider the source." The old saying "Keep your friends close and your enemies closer" is a precaution to stay guarded in our dealings with unreasonable people.

"Blitzkrieg" was the term developed during World War II that described the fast-paced, mobilized assault tactics used by the German army. After using Blitzkrieg to conquer Poland to the east, the Germans turned to the west and prepared for attack. During these months of battle preparation, few shots were being fired. Day-to-day life was largely unchanged, and many Western Europeans almost forgot there was a war. Someone coined the term "Sitzkrieg" to describe this period in which people sat and enjoyed their business-as-usual lives. One of the confounding things about unreasonable people is that they can be difficult sometimes but normal at others, which leaves us perplexed. We need to guard against being lulled into complacency by periods of normalcy. The dysfunction of Level 2 unreasonable people will show up later if not sooner. We shouldn't allow Sitzkrieg to fool us into thinking there will be no more Blitzkrieg.

Be Firm

In Chapter 7 we discussed ways to resist drama enticements. Often it's best to use *passive resistance* methods—ignoring the enticement keeps us out of the drama. At other times *active resistance* is necessary, the chief characteristic of which is the word "no." Both methods have their place. Solomon, the writer of Ecclesiastes, said that there is a "time to be silent and a time to speak."[1] English philosopher Edmund Burke said, "The only thing necessary for the triumph of evil is for good men to do nothing."[2] Clearly there are times in which speaking up and saying no is the only way to contain the effects of an unreasonable person's pathology. Examples of active resistance include:

- refusing to allow a classmate to cheat off your paper
- refusing to pass on gossip
- calling someone's bluff
- finding various ways to communicate "that's none of your business"
- telling the person that what he's doing is wrong and to stop it
- refusing to enable bad behavior
- explaining the consequences for bad behavior: "I won't have this conversation if you continue swearing at me."
- allowing a person to experience the consequences of bad behavior (also known as "giving him enough rope to hang himself")

• using the legal system to force compliance with contracts or agreements

Undoubtedly there are many examples, all of which communicate "No!" Henry Cloud and John Townsend, in their excellent books on boundaries, discuss in detail when to say yes and when to say no.[3]

Not surprisingly, the unreasonable person doesn't like resistance of any sort. If we employ the "no" approach, we can expect him to:

• falsely accuse us

• criticize us

• impugn our motives

• shift the subject to our faults

• try harder to entice us

• elicit others to take his side against us

• remain clueless about the reasons for our resistance

When the Level 1 hits boundaries, he gets frustrated but eventually responds to the frustration by growing. When the Level 2 hits boundaries, he gets frustrated, hits them repeatedly, gets frustrated repeatedly, but will eventually adjust to the boundaries to avoid further frustration. His behavior may change in a positive direction—but not due to personal growth. Instead it's just to avoid personal frustration. He may change his behavior without changing his heart, but the change of behavior for any reason makes his relationship with us easier for us to tolerate.

A client of mine had a husband who was known publicly as a happy, wonderful churchman but known privately by his wife and children as a profane, controlling jerk. For years she argued for change but repeatedly found herself reasoning with an unreasonable person. For instance, as they would go through the serving line at church for a fellowship meal, he would quietly snipe at her, demean her, and swear at her about being too slow, too picky, and so forth. But when they got to the table, he became joyfully engaging, entertaining the people around them with funny stories. This hypocritical display of phony spirituality and his unwillingness to acknowledge it made her sick. On the way to church one day, she calmly said, "I need you to understand something. If you cuss at me when we're going through the dinner line, I'll sit at another table. I just want you to know in advance." He barked back that he had no idea what she was talking about. But when they went through the line, he was nicer to her.

Why was he nicer? It wasn't because he had a sudden infusion of awareness, humility, empathy, or any of those things. None of those muscles grew. He was nicer because he was image conscious. He wanted to avoid the embarrassment of explaining why his wife was sitting at a different table. He did the right thing for the wrong reasons. But doing the right thing for any reason made that aspect of living with him a little easier.

Be Insulated

We can take hot baked potatoes from the oven, but we better wear oven mitts. We can go for walks in Antarctica, but we better wear heavy coats. Insulation makes it possible for us to handle things that would otherwise harm us. Since the Level 2 unreasonable person can inflict emotional harm, we need insulation or "thicker skin." If we're thin-skinned, the person "gets to us" or "gets under our skin." He or she has the power to drive us crazy, wear us out, make us sick, and generally dominate the landscape of our lives. I often hear clients say something like, "I'm sick and tired of (the unreasonable person) renting all the space in my brain."

To keep this from happening, we need to develop thicker skin through a combination of exposure, drama avoidance, and time. If you've ever played a guitar, you know your fingers hurt when you first start holding down the strings. But the more you do it, the less it hurts because you build up calluses. Relational calluses develop through exposure to the unreasonable person. But the only way the exposure helps is when we resist being enticed into drama participation, like we discussed in Chapter 7. Our skin thickens as we repeatedly avoid enticements.

In some cases, insulation comes from geography—distancing ourselves from the person. In Charles Dickens' *A Christmas Carol,* the Ghost of Christmas Past reminds Scrooge of his previous bad choices, the chief of which was placing his greedy ambitions above his engagement to a wonderful girl. After realizing the destructiveness of this relationship, the fair young lady makes these statements.

> Another idol has displaced me…I have seen your nobler aspirations fall off one by one, until the master passion, Gain, engrosses you, have I not?…That which promised happiness when we were one in heart is fraught with misery now that we are two. How often and how keenly I have thought of this, I will not say. It is enough that I have thought of it, and I can release you…May you be happy in the life you have chosen. She left him, and they parted.[4]

Like the woman in Dickens' story, there are times when it's necessary to distance ourselves from an unreasonable person. But when life requires us to live with or work in close quarters with the person, an emotional coat must be worn. Developing thicker skin enables people to say, "He doesn't get to me like he used to." Most often, the unreasonable person doesn't change a bit. What changes is the power of that person's pathology to affect our lives. With thicker skin, he or she may still irritate us, but he or she can no longer devastate us.

Be Encouraged to Stay Sane

When we have to deal with an unreasonable person who is determined not to change, we may start feeling a little crazy ourselves. Remember, his survival depends on getting us to believe there's nothing wrong with him, but there's definitely something wrong with us. If that projection from the outside resonates with our insides, we internalize it, start to believe it, and feel crazy.

The only way to keep this projective process from succeeding is to listen to other voices—people on the outside who know us, understand us, and believe in us. When we internalize their encouragement, we gain the needed strength to counteract the projections. Courage is then brought inside—"in couragement," if you will. We need people who communicate, "Don't forget: You're not the crazy one. You're just a normally flawed person who needs to resist playing your role in that person's drama."

Setting Boundaries with Level 3 (Dangerous) Unreasonable People

If it seems necessary to him, the Level 3 unreasonable person will hurt or eliminate his opposition in order to win, so conflict with him has the potential of being physically dangerous. In some cases he may be a danger to himself. So we must give priority to boundaries that maintain *safety*. Safety boundaries result from being strong, wise, and distant.

Be Strong

Our goal with a Level 3 unreasonable person is safety, which is only achievable through strong security measures. I began this chapter by explaining the "peace through strength" approach used by the United States in dealing with the Soviet Union. On a personal level, such measures may include the following.

Law Enforcement

Law enforcement officials exist "to protect and to serve." If physical safety is being threatened, we may have to call the police, have orders of protection issued, and file charges. In response, our Level 3 opponent may pose less of a threat for self-serving reasons—to avoid legal consequences.

Self-Protection

Safety may be increased through common-sense protective measures such as deadbolts, security systems, and fences. Being trained in self-defense techniques may sometimes be prudent.

Risk Exposure

Here's what we want a dangerous person to think: *It's too risky for me to attack you.* That's one reason why people jog with dogs—so that potential muggers will see the dog and be disinclined to attack. Exposure to risk (the dog) contributes to safety. The thinking behind the policy of "Mutually Assured Destruction" (MAD) was "The assurance of the Soviet Union's destruction will deter it from launching a nuclear first strike." The world was safer with this policy in place until a much better system replaced it—the ending of the Cold War.

Be Wise

The consequences of acting foolishly are greater with a Level 3 unreasonable person—it may cost us our lives. Therefore it is imperative that our actions be governed by wisdom.

Avoid provocations. We use various phrases to express this, including: "Don't poke a hornet's nest" or, in reference to snakes, "If you don't bother it, it won't bother you." We should be careful not to say, "I know what you're up to, and you won't get away with it." Such provocations only provide an incentive to the unreasonable person to "win"—which may include hurting us.

My very first client as a graduate student was a pleasant-yet-scary young man who told me about being angry with his employer. When I asked him how angry he was, he replied, "Oh, I've had him in my sights." Being very green, I said, "I'm not so sure I believe you." In response, he produced a revolver and declared, "Now do you believe me?" I did. And I became a little wiser that day about avoiding provocations.

Avoid disclosure. A poker phrase used to express this idea is "Don't tip your hand." Don't tell a dangerous unreasonable person about the weapons in your arsenal. For instance, it may not be wise for a woman to announce to her physically abusive husband her plans to leave and stay with a friend. If she were to do so, he could thwart her exit by disabling the automobile or doing something worse.

Be distant. Sometimes a dangerous person will respect the law in order to avoid legal consequences. But there are times when he may violate a restraining order. I'm sure you've read about situations like this in the news. In such cases, maintaining distance from that person may be the only way to keep safe.

The house in which I grew up was located next to a creek, which served as a haven for venomous snakes that often slithered into our yard. I hate snakes, so to safeguard myself from these reptiles, I avoided certain parts of the yard during the summer months, using distance as a buffer between them and me. Achieving safety with a dangerous person may require us to do that at times, such as:

- breaking off contact with the person
- not placing ourselves in situations where physical safety is jeopardized
- leaving the premises where danger exists
- calling the police to have a dangerous person escorted from the premises

Be Encouraged to Stay Safe

I've had clients involved in "nitroglycerin" relationships where one misstep could shake the bottle and cause a deadly explosion. They've become so wrapped up in the drama that they've lost sight of the potential danger. Remember, we tend to not deal well with unreasonable people in isolation because we can get lulled into complacency. We need the support and perspective that others provide. With dangerous people, others help us by:

- providing safe havens if and when they are needed
- reminding us not to take unnecessary risks
- providing reality checks should we lose perspective concerning the danger

When Patti Set Relational Boundaries

Patti's mom wasn't physically dangerous, but she sure could do a number on Patti's emotions. Patti came to realize that Mom could affect her only to the extent that she allowed her to do so. She couldn't change Mom, but she could change the boundaries so that momma drama had less of an impact on her and her family's day-to-day lives. Patti hated the fact that her mom was such a drama queen, so she kept giving her more chances than she deserved to relate reasonably. But Mom proved herself time and again to be a determined martyr who demanded caretaking from others, particularly Patti. It was a bitter pill to swallow, but Patti had to adjust her expectations—from hoping Mom would change to always anticipating the martyr role. Often she would say to me, "I feel like there's something wrong with me for having such negative thoughts about my mother," to which I would reply, "There would be something wrong with you if you didn't think this way because your thoughts reflect reality. You're not being critical but realistic."

As unfamiliar as it was, she started saying no to her mom, declining unreasonable requests and refusing to take guilt trips. For instance, Patti would calmly answer appeals for late-night emergency drugstore runs with statements such as, "Mom, it's late and we're not going out for that. You'll either have to pick it up yourself tonight or in the morning." Predictably, Mom would get upset and say, "Well, I'd go if I were young like you and had a body that worked. If only you had an idea of what this is like for me. But I know you need your sleep, so I'll just have to figure it out myself." Note the projection attempt: "You're being selfish." In response, Patti learned to say, "OK. I better run. Talk to you later." She would then hang up the phone. Patti also learned not to give reasons for declining because her mom would always explain why those reasons weren't valid.

This wasn't easy for Patti because she felt mean—like she was disobeying one of the Ten Commandments, "Honor your father and mother." In fact, she wasn't being mean, just clear. And it honored her mom more to stop enabling her bad behavior and to contain the effects of that behavior on the innocent bystanders—her husband and children.

When Patti realized just how much time and energy had been spent on the mom problem, she started limiting the length and frequency of their visits. She dealt with her anger at Alexander Graham Bell by limiting their phone calls and allowing the answering machine to take messages more often. And to handle the multiple frantic messages her mom would often leave, Patti familiarized herself with her machine's delete button. She felt bad about this at first but got used to it. She also agreed with Bill to limit the amount of time devoted to drama analysis. Lengthy rehearsals of her mom's latest audacious intrusions did no good and deprived them of energy that could be devoted to raising their two children.

It also helped Patti to compare notes with a few trusted friends who were in similar situations. It encouraged her and made her feel less crazy to hear that others were going through some of the same things. She also noticed just how many movies and sitcoms had story lines about people who were being driven batty by crazy people. It was funnier on TV than it was in real life, but it did help to laugh whenever possible.

This chart summarizes boundary considerations with the three levels of unreasonable people.

Boundaries with Unreasonable People

	Level One (Dormant)	Level Two (Determined)	Level Three (Dangerous)
Goal	Growth	Containment	Safety
Boundary setting	Be frustrating Be persistent Be patient Be encouraged (to stay with it)	Be expectant Be firm Be insulated Be encouraged (to stay sane)	Be strong Be wise Be distant Be encouraged (to stay safe)

Acknowledge Relational Realities

Another main aspect of limit acceptance is to realize certain realities that must characterize relationships with unreasonable people.

A Relationship with Limited Depth

Our relationships with some unreasonable people may be workable only if the level of relationship is limited. It may be more superficial than we'd prefer, but *superficial and civil is better than close and contentious*. I've had many clients over the years like Patti, who struggle with relating to an unreasonable parent. The parent may be a master, messiah, martyr, or mute, and the adult child is expected to play his or her role in the drama, the unspoken message being, "If you play your role, we'll get along just fine." If drama enticements are resisted, the relationship changes. In some cases, refusing a role in the drama ends the relationship. But more often, it changes the level of closeness. One client put it this way:

> I can still relate to her but I've had to forfeit the idea of closeness. If "1" is the most superficial and "10" is the deepest, I have to limit my relationship with her to the 1 to 3 range. It's not deep, but it's still a relationship. By confining it to the levels that are possible, I get to have a relationship without forfeiting my sanity.

Relating in this way may feel disingenuous to some of us, like we're pretending to get along when we're really not. Actually, it's more honest to be superficial if relating more deeply requires drama participation.

A Relationship with Limited Value

Experiencing dilemmas in our relationships with unreasonable people is not unusual. On the one hand we greatly value their gifts, talents, and abilities. On the other hand, they drive us nuts. We treasure their talents but deplore the drama. It's like having a brilliant physician with a horrible bedside manner. We can't stand him personally but wouldn't want anyone else to perform the surgery.

We may have unreasonable people relationships that are valuable to us in some ways but detrimental in others. When this is the case, we can restructure the relationship to make the most of its limited value. We can't "make a silk purse out of a sow's ear," as the saying goes, but we may be able to "make a pretty good tote bag." [5] The relationship may not be all that we desire, but it has value to us nonetheless.

A Relationship with Limited Growth

One of the outcomes of good conflict with unreasonable people is that we grow whether they do or not. We become better versions of ourselves, while they remain unchanged or become worse versions. The growth is limited to us.

The 1980 movie *Ordinary People* won the Academy Award for Best Picture. It tells the story of a family that appears to be quite ordinary. Beneath this facade of normality, however, bubbles a witch's brew of dysfunction. The witch stirring the cauldron is the mom, a Level 2 master named Beth. Beth has little tolerance for anything that's not spotless, perfect, and trouble free—which includes her less-than-perfect son, Conrad. Conrad is struggling to find his place in a family where Buck, his greatly revered (perfect) brother, died in an accident. Beth resents Conrad because he's not perfect like Buck. She continually seems to suggest that the wrong son died. Beth projects her negatives onto Conrad, who is made out to be the crazy one—the source of all that's wrong in the family. The dad, Calvin, is the good-natured sort who views the world through rose-colored glasses, rendering him oblivious to the dysfunction swirling around him. Calvin misses it, but Conrad desperately needs him to see it.

Throughout the movie Conrad seeks help from someone who does see it—his therapist. He also has a friend who sees it and believes in him as a person. With their help and encouragement, Conrad does the hard work required of someone growing and seeking truth, which he finds to be liberating yet excruciating.

Toward the movie's end, Calvin finally emerges from his oblivion and notices what Conrad has seen all along—the witch stirring the cauldron. He verbalizes his newfound realization to Beth, who predictably denies any wrongdoing. So determined is she to maintain her rightness that she severs ties with the family, leaving Calvin and Conrad stunned and saddened. Conrad, it turns out, was the sane one while Beth was the crazy one. Calvin was sane too, though it took him a while to come to grips with what he'd been ignoring. The movie ends on a note that is simultaneously tragic and hopeful. It was tragic for Beth, who remained stubbornly stuck in her pathology. It was hopeful for Conrad and Calvin, who grew as a result of facing some difficult realities. They became better versions of themselves.

When a reasonable person has good conflict with an unreasonable person, the reasonable person grows even though the unreasonable person fails to do so—unless he's a Level 1. Good conflict, even with an unreasonable person, contributes to the growth of our character and identity. It brings out our best; we become better versions of ourselves.

When Patti Acknowledged Relational Realities

Patti lamented the fact that her relationship with her mother could never be deep. The price she paid for closeness was too expensive for her and too costly for the ones who legitimately required Patti's time and energy. Patti's relationship with her mom couldn't be deep, but it could be doable as long as it was more superficial. She couldn't make it work on all the levels because some of those levels required drama participation. But a limited relationship, she felt, was better than no relationship, and her mom would accept whatever level of closeness Patti was willing to allow—even though that couldn't be defined openly. Patti was fortunate because the stance of some unreasonable people is "relate my way or no way." Beth, the mom in *Ordinary People,* was one of those.

Patti hated having to limit the relationship because her mom had some truly admirable traits. She was a wonderful grandmother, and the kids loved being around her. She was well read, she had a great sense of history, she could tell interesting stories, she was a talented artist, she was well-liked by others, and she could make a mean pot of chili. The ongoing challenge for Patti was how to enjoy the good while screening out the bad. She got to where she could do this pretty well.

When Patti did all that was required to have good conflict, her mom hadn't changed a bit and was exactly the same as before. But learning to deal with her mom in a healthier way made Patti healthier. She grew a lot despite the fact that her mother was still a child inhabiting the body of an adult.

Patti and Her Mom's Relationship Now

Patti's form of good conflict was different from Neil and Laura's, where conflict problems were solved in a mutually agreeable way. In Patti's case, the problems weren't so much solved as they were "restrained" so her family wouldn't be dominated by them. It would be pushing it too far to say that Patti now feels good about the relationship with her mom. She does feel good about some parts of it, but, more accurately, she feels stronger, having previously felt powerless to do anything to make things better. Her depression, which resulted from momma drama, lifted when she became more adept at avoiding the theatrics.

In many ways Patti is wiser about people. She used to give everyone the benefit of the doubt, assuming that reasonable treatment would guarantee reciprocal reasonable treatment. She now understands that everyone is not like that. Some people simply don't have it in them to relate reasonably, a difficult reality to accept when one of those people is your mother.

An unexpected side effect of learning to do conflict the good way was the development of a "sixth sense" about unreasonable people. Patti has intuitive hunches at times that a seemingly reasonable person is actually an unreasonable wolf in reasonable sheep's clothing. More often than not, her hunches prove to be right.

Patti now has a healthy relationship with her mom that's not contingent upon her mom being healthy. It works because of the effort Patti put in to make it workable.

In a Nutshell

To have good conflict with unreasonable people, we have to understand them, avoid their dramas, and accept the limits that must characterize our relationships with them. This involves setting relational boundaries, which should foster growth with Level 1s, provide containment with Level 2s, and ensure safety with Level 3s. We also acknowledge that relationships with unreasonable people will have limited depth, limited value, and limited growth.

For Reflection

1. Why are boundaries necessary in relationships with unreasonable people?

2. Why are supportive relationships so important in helping you deal well with unreasonable people?

3. Why is it necessary to be patient? To be firm?

4. What is the primary goal of conflict with a Level 1 unreasonable person?

With a Level 2?

With a Level 3?

5. Explain the limitations that characterize unreasonable person relationships. Why is the relationship limited in these ways?

THE REPAIR SHOP

Early on we discussed a universal human dilemma: We love closeness but hate the problems that sometimes accompany closeness. Connection brings conflict, and our flaws cause friction. So having good relationships requires us to handle friction in a good way, even though we're not always inclined to do so.

We're all imperfect people living in a world with imperfect others. But there was a time when perfection ruled the day. People never argued, they didn't irritate each other, and the term "people problems" would have drawn blank stares. The first three chapters of the Bible describe that time, which took place in a Garden. The two inhabitants enjoyed a period of perfect peace and harmony that ended when their bad decisions got them kicked out of the neighborhood. If we skip ahead to the Bible's last three chapters, we read about a future age when people will be liberated from their imperfections. The setting is a City that will last forever. Imagine that. No buttons getting pushed, no overreactions, no arguments to work out, no amends to make, no jerks driving us crazy—for eternity. Imperfection entered the world when the Garden Club members blew it, and it will be eradicated one day when the only Perfect One returns to reign in the City.

But sandwiched between the Garden and the City is what we might call the Repair Shop, a place where broken people are currently being refurbished. The Repairman has a very interesting method of renovation. He uses close-contact friction to smooth out flaws and knock off rough edges. As we know, friction can be good and bad. A piece of sandpaper rubbed against a fine piece of wood enhances its beauty, but a grain of sand rubbing against an eyeball can cause blindness. This particular Repairman is all about good friction, using the abrasive action generated in close connections to shape people and grow them into better versions of themselves. In fact, the sign above his door reads, "No friction, no growth."

While many topics are discussed between the Bible's opening and closing chapters, getting along with others is a recurring theme. Certain books of the Bible contain "wisdom literature," which puts forth timeless tenets for wise living. As a general rule, life works better when these principles are followed. One of the books, Proverbs, has much to say about human relationships. Written almost 3,000 years ago, all the elements we've been discussing in this book are there—bad conflict, good conflict, reasonableness, and unreasonableness. So the issues we've been dealing with have been around for a long time. The labels may be modern, but the concepts are ancient.

In this brief review of handling people problems, we'll take a look at what the writers of Proverbs had to say about relationships. They said a lot so we'll only be able to look at a representative sampling of verses.

Bad Conflict

People problems started not long after the Garden party was over, as noted in Genesis 3. One of the inhabitants' sons killed his brother, and people have been clashing ever since. When human nature rules the conflict process, things seldom go well. A fight (tiger) reaction is being described when a Proverbs writer states, "Hot tempers start fights."[1] But we're also told that flight (turtle) reactions don't help either: "A spoken reprimand is better than approval that's never expressed."[2]

Even delicious food won't counteract the bad feelings associated with poorly handled conflict: "A meal of bread and water in contented peace is better than a banquet spiced with quarrels."[3] Nor will plush living conditions make up for the awful feelings: "Better to live alone in a tumbledown shack than share a mansion with a nagging spouse."[4] Referring to something that sounds like Chinese water torture, one proverb says, "A nagging spouse is like the drip, drip, drip of a leaky faucet; you can't turn it off, and you can't get away from it."[5] Bad conflict is certain to negatively impact relationships. A Proverbs writer tells us about seven things God hates and singles out the last one that he "loathes with a passion": "a troublemaker in the family."[6] The word *family* refers to people who are biologically related but also may include groupings of friends as well. Clearly God has a particular distaste for the far-reaching, destructive effects of bad conflict on relationships. And when bad conflict governs how we relate, it brings out our worst. One proverb tells us, "The hotheaded do things they'll later regret."[7]

Good Conflict

We discovered earlier that the best alternative to either a fight or flight reaction is honest, civil conversation—a *chosen* response. This seems to be what one Proverbs writer means when he says, "Hot tempers start fights; a calm, cool spirit keeps the peace."[8] Those who avoid bad conflict and adopt good conflict methods are commended: "It's a mark of good character to avert quarrels, but fools love to pick fights."[9] When people handle conflict well, they forge the ability to form close, lasting relationships. We're told, "Do a favor and win a friend forever; nothing can untie that bond."[10] The Repairman's use of relational friction as a means of molding us shows up when we read, "You use steel to sharpen steel, and one friend sharpens another."[11] We're also told, "In the end, serious reprimand is appreciated far more than bootlicking flattery."[12] Friction may sometimes hurt, but it serves a good purpose in good conflict.

Reasoning with the Reasonable

Proverbs writers, who refer to reasonable people using terms such as "wise" and "prudent," don't specifically mention "reason muscles," but they do discuss the qualities needed to handle personal wrongness.

Humility is frequently emphasized: "Don't assume that you know it all"[13] and "Pride first, then the crash, but humility is precursor to honor."[14] *Awareness* seems to be in view when we read, "Ears that hear and eyes that see—we get our basic equipment from GOD."[15] Taking *responsibility* for personal wrongness is spoken of: "Welcoming correction is a mark of good sense"[16] and "Listen to good advice if you want to live well."[17] Morning people could use this admonition: "If you wake up your friend early in the morning by shouting 'Rise and shine!' it will sound to him more like a curse than a blessing."[18] We're being told to have some *empathy* for others. Finally, *reliability* is spoken of: "A quiet rebuke to a person of good sense does more than a whack on the head of a fool."[19] That means the wise person will take action on making changes in his or her life when necessary.

We're told, "The start of a quarrel is like a leak in a dam, so stop it before it bursts."[20] To flee the trap of bad conflict, we break the cycle at one of three places. First, we must *keep our buttons from getting pushed.* Understanding our buttons may be what is being discussed in "keep vigilant watch over your heart."[21] Remember, buttons can be pushed just as easily by perceptions as they can by actual pushes. Perhaps that's why these proverbs say, "Answering before listening is both stupid and rude"[22] and "Don't jump to conclusions—there may be a perfectly good explanation for what you just saw."[23]

The book of Proverbs says a lot about the second place to break the cycle—*responding rather than reacting.* "A gentle response defuses anger."[24] Responding civilly versus impulsively displaying anger is also spoken of: "Slowness to anger makes for deep understanding; a quick-tempered person stockpiles stupidity."[25] Keeping our words in check is mentioned: "The one who knows much says little; an understanding person remains calm. Even dunces who keep quiet are thought to be wise; as long as they keep their mouths shut, they're smart."[26]

The last way to break the bad conflict cycle is by *refraining from pushing buttons:* "A sharp tongue kindles a temper-fire."[27] Not pushing someone else's buttons has a constructive outcome: "Gentle speech breaks down rigid defenses."[28]

If we flex our muscles and flee the trap, we can fix the problems that caused the conflict. The writers of Proverbs don't lay it out the way I did in Chapter 5. And yet the ideas I presented are in line with the philosophy of Proverbs. Nothing will get solved if we argue about everything at once. We must take care to understand each others' views, which fits in with the *empathy* verses we just read. We must agree on a solution that comes closest to meeting both sets of interests. One of the solutions we discussed was healthy deferring, which seems to be suggested in "overlook an offense and bond a friendship; fasten on to a slight and—good-bye friend."[29] Next, we must plan specifically how to implement our solution and then check to make sure it comes to pass. This specific process isn't mentioned but the outcome is described: "Just as lotions and fragrance give sensual delight, a sweet friendship refreshes the soul."[30] Solving people problems enables us to enjoy the benefits that we seek from close connections!

Dealing with the Unreasonable

Just as we have uncomplimentary terms for unreasonable people, so do the writers of Proverbs. Theirs include: fools, scoffers, evil, schemers, slanderers, scorners, unjust, gossips, rebels, proud, and haughty. The proverbs frequently draw contrasts between wise people and foolish people and suggest that we handle them differently. The fact that the book of Proverbs places so much emphasis on friendship and interaction with people tells us how important it is to guard against the influence of the foolish.

The book of Proverbs helps us understand foolish people and warns us about them. From the verses listed previously, we know fools have atrophied "reason muscles": humility, awareness, responsibility, empathy, and reliability. They entice us into drama participation: "Dear friend, if bad companions tempt you, don't go along with them"[31] and, warning against being enticed by a seductress or desperate housewife, "Keep your distance from such a woman; absolutely stay out of her neighborhood."[32] Unreasonable people confuse us, sicken us, and exhaust us. We're told, "Carrying a log across your shoulders while you're hefting a boulder with your arms is nothing compared to the burden of putting up with a fool."[33]

We can't reason with unreasonable people, and attempting to do so sucks us into drama participation, which we're instructed to avoid: "If you reason with an arrogant cynic, you'll get slapped in the face."[34] We avoid dramas by keeping our distance from them,[35] refusing to reason with them,[36] refusing to place our trust in them,[37] and by refusing to envy them when things seem to go their way.[38] And if they ever seem to be paying no price for their misdeeds, we must remind ourselves that justice is handled by God: "Don't ever say, 'I'll get you for that!' Wait for GOD; he'll settle the score."[39]

Many years after the book of Proverbs was written, Jesus had an encounter that is mentioned in John 8. He met with some Pharisees, the unreasonable people of his day. They asked him a question designed as a trap—whatever answer he gave could be used against him. Instead of answering their question, he stooped down and began drawing in the dust. When they realized they weren't going to get an answer, they left. Perhaps this was a drama staged and a drama avoided. Understanding that they weren't interested in a reasonable answer, Jesus refused to bite the bait and get sucked into participation.

Let's recap. In the early pages of this book, we talked about a dilemma that confronts us all. That is, we desire closeness but deplore what closeness brings—problems. The porcupine dance is a metaphor describing how we try to resolve the dilemma, moving in to find intimacy and moving out to avoid pain. But the dance doesn't resolve the dilemma, it perpetuates it. The only way the dilemma is resolved is by solving the inevitable people problems. Like porcupines relaxing their quills, fixing problems with people gives us a way to be close to people without experiencing constant pain. But we're not naturally good at it, tending toward bad conflict. Good conflict can be learned, but we have to know what to do *and* practice doing it. Good conflict methods with reasonable people are quite different from the ones used with those who are unreasonable.

In closing, I'd like to say three more things. First, there is a way of thinking that pushes my buttons: "If you follow these simple steps, your problem will be solved." This attractive and compelling notion is used to sell a wide array of products that promise to produce washboard abs without exercise, reduce fat without effort, and generate wealth without discipline. This idea is found in many "how to" books that purport to contain the keys, the secrets, and the quick-and-easy steps to solving some particularly thorny problem. Changing bad conflict into good is neither simple nor easy, but it is achievable if we know what to do and practice what we know. The outcome is worth the time and effort required to achieve good conflict. All of the results of good conflict are good.

Second, I have some good news and some bad news. The good news is that good conflict is achievable. The bad news is that we will continue to make mistakes. "Good enough" is possible, but "perfection" is not. The gravitational pull surrounding the conflict trap is enormous, and we'll find ourselves sucked in to old patterns of button pushing and reacting from time to time. Our heads will tell us to go in one direction while our impulses pull us in another. Falling back into the conflict trap is not a problem—but staying there is.

Third, I've related what I've seen work and not work when it comes to relationships and conflicts. I've offered a fresh look at what we know about conflict, placing it in a different big-picture framework than usual. Viewed from this perspective, hopefully the truisms and rules are more understandable and useful to you. Knowledge helps because we can line ourselves up with what's true. "Fair fighting" rules work because they instruct us how to act without perpetuating conflict when conflict happens.

If you're a porcupine reading this book, relax your quills and nuzzle up close to your partner. For the rest of you, implementing the suggestions in this book will help you have healthier, more fulfilling relationships and promote your growth into a better you.

Bad Conflict
The Conflict Trap

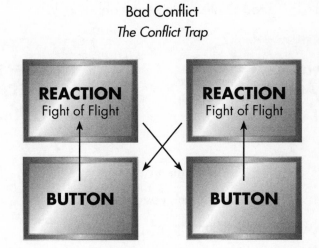

No problems are solved.

It feels awful.

Relationships become alienated.

It brings out your worst.

(See chapter 2 for more details.)

Good Conflict with Reasonable People

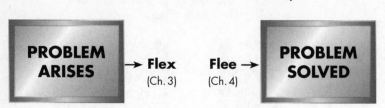

Problems are solved.

It feels positive.

Relationships become closer.

It brings out your best.

Good Conflict with Unreasonable People

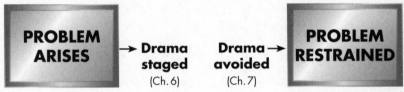

Problems are restrained.

It feels empowering.

Relationships can be good but limited.

It brings out your best.

You grow; he or she may not grow.

NOTES

Chapter 1: Dealing with Porcupines

1. John Ortberg, *Everybody's Normal Till You Get to Know Them* (Grand Rapids, MI: Zondervan, 2003), p. 22.

Chapter 2: The Conflict Trap

1. Gregory Lester, *Power with People* (Buena Vista, CO: Ashcroft Press, 1995), p. 33.
2. Ibid., p. 46.
3. Ortberg, *Everybody's Normal,* p. 22.
4. Nicholas Hall, "Embracing Conflict" (Celebration, FL: Health Dateline, n.d.), cassettetapes.
5. William Butler Yeats, although it might be from his father, John Butler Yeats.

Section 2: Reasoning with the Reasonable

1. Howard Hendricks, "The Best of Prof" (Dallas, TX: Howard G. Hendricks Center for Christian Leadership, (2005), CD series.

Chapter 3: Flexing the Muscles

1. Stephen R. Covey, *The Seven Habits of Highly Successful People* (New York: Simon & Schuster, 1989), p. 235.
2. Paul Tournier, *To Understand Each Other* (Richmond, VA: John Knox Press, 1962), p. 29.

Chapter 4: Fleeing the Trap

1. C.S. Lewis, radio adaptation of Lewis' inaugural lecture as professor of Medieval and Renaissance Literature at Cambridge University, 1954.
2. Dudley Weeks, Ph.D., *Eight Essential Steps to Conflict Resolution* (New York: Penguin Putnam, Inc., 1992), p. 90.

Chapter. 5: Fixing the Problems

1. Gary Lacefield, "Mediation Certification Program," American Association of Christian Counselors, 2004, p. 3.
2. W.T. Fisher and M.C. Ury, *Getting to Yes* (Harrisonburg, VA: R.R. Donnelly & Sons Company, 1981).
3. Susan M. Heitler, *From Conflict to Resolution* (New York: W.W. Norton & Company, 1990), p. 24.
4. Hall, "Embracing Conflict."

Chapter 6: Assessing the Opposition

1. Joyce Landorf Heatherly, *Irregular People* (Austin, TX: Balcony Publishing, 1982).

2. Susan Forward, *Emotional Blackmail* (New York: HarperCollins Publishing, 1997).

3. Henry Cloud and John Townsend, *Safe People* (Grand Rapids, MI: Zondervan, 1995).

4. Scott Peck, *People of the Lie* (New York: Simon and Schuster, 1983).

5. Howard Hendricks, *Leadership and Motivation* (San Bernardino, CA: Campus Crusade for Christ, 1972), cassettetape series.

6. Gregory W. Lester, Ph.D., *Personality Disorders in Social Work & Health Care* (Nashville: Cross Country University, 1999), p. 24.

7. Ibid.

8. Sheldon Cashdan, Ph.D., *Object Relations Therapy* (New York: W.W. Norton & Company, 1988), p. 64.

9. Ibid., p. 74.

10. Ibid., p. 61.

11. Peck, *People of the Lie,* p. 66.

12. Lester, *Personality Disorders.*

13. David Brinkley, *Washington Goes to War* (New York: Ballantine Books, 1988).

Chapter 7: Avoiding the Drama

1. M. St. Clair, *Object Relations and Self Psychology: An Introduction* (Monterey, CA: Brooks/Cole Publishing Company, 1986), p. 60.

2. Lester, *Personality Disorders,* p. 32.

3. Rudyard Kipling, "If," a poem that first appeared in his collection "Rewards and Fairies," 1909.

Chapter 8: Accepting the Limits

1. Ecclesiastes 3:7.

2. Edmund Burke, "Thoughts on the Cause of Present Discontents," paraphrased.

3. Henry Cloud and John Townsend, *Boundaries* (Grand Rapids, MI: Zondervan, 1992); Henry Cloud and John Townsend, *Boundaries in Marriage* (Grand Rapids, MI: Zondervan, 1999); Henry Cloud and John Townsend, *Boundaries in Dating* (Grand Rapids, MI: Zondervan, 2000); Henry Cloud and John Townsend, *Boundaries with Kids* (Grand Rapids, MI: Zondervan, 1998).

4. Charles Dickens, *A Christmas Carol and Other Christmas Stories* (New York: Penguin Books USA, Inc., 1984), pp. 72-74.

5. D.R. Harvey, *A Change of Heart* (Grand Rapids, MI: Baker Book House, 1993).

The Repair Shop

1. Proverbs 15:18.
2. Proverbs 27:5.
3. Proverbs 17:1.
4. Proverbs 21:9.
5. Proverbs 27:15-16.
6. Proverbs 6:16,19.
7. Proverbs 14:17.
8. Proverbs 15:18.
9. Proverbs 20:3.
10. Proverbs 18:19.
11. Proverbs 27:17.
12. Proverbs 28:23.
13. Proverbs 3:7.
14. Proverbs 18:12.
15. Proverbs 20:12.
16. Proverbs 15:5.
17. Proverbs 15:31.
18. Proverbs 27:14.
19. Proverbs 17:10.
20. Proverbs 17:14.
21. Proverbs 4:23.
22. Proverbs 18:13.
23. Proverbs 25:8.
24. Proverbs 15:1.
25. Proverbs 14:29.
26. Proverbs 17:27-28.
27. Proverbs 15:1.
28. Proverbs 25:15.
29. Proverbs 17:9
30. Proverbs 27:9.
31. Proverbs 1:10.
32. Proverbs 5:8.
33. Proverbs 27:3.
34. Proverbs 9:7.
35. Proverbs 24:1.
36. Proverbs 26:4-5.
37. Proverbs 20:19.
38. Proverbs 23:17-18; 24:1-2.
39. Proverbs 20:22.

GLOSSARY

Awareness muscle: The reasoning ability that enables us to be aware of personal shortcomings.

Bad conflict: Conflict we experience when our energies are spent on button pushing and reacting instead of problem solving.

Button: Places where we feel insecure, weak, overly sensitized, or easily threatened.

Compromise: Each side gives up something to reach a satisfactory conflict solution.

Conceptual threat: The emotional threat experienced from a suggestion that something is wrong with us.

Conflict trap: Another term for *bad conflict.* The cycle of reacting to each other's reactions. It's called a trap because it's easy to fall into and hard to escape.

Containment boundaries: Limitations we create to contain the disruptive influence of a determined (level 2) unreasonable person.

Dangerous: Unreasonable people who safeguard their need for rightness through any means possible, including force.

Debriefing: A healthy "after argument" process to evaluate what happened and assess what can be done to correct any errors in future arguments.

Deferring: Willingly laying aside our preferences as a way to achieve a conflict solution. Deferring may be healthy or unhealthy.

Determined: Unreasonable people who respond to conflict by stiffening their resolve to win. As a result of conflict, they become worse versions of themselves.

Dormant: Unreasonable people who respond to conflict by growing. They become better versions of themselves.

Drama: Unreasonable people's alternative to problem solving. Their ability to perform roles is contingent upon getting others to play their roles.

Empathy muscle: The reasoning ability that enables us to be bothered if our wrongness hurts others.

Enticement: The process that induces us to play a role in an unreasonable person's drama.

Fight reaction: Aggressive response to a problem that displays through audible and visible attacks, such as insults, yelling, slamming doors.

Flight reaction: "Run away" response to a problem revealed subtly through withdrawals that are often felt more than observed, such as avoidance, changing the subject, or freeze-outs.

Good conflict: Problem-solving process that enables a good outcome. With reasonable people, good conflict results in problem solving. With unreasonable people, good conflict results in problem restraint.

Growth boundaries: Limitations that result in growth for a dormant (level 1) unreasonable person.

Humility muscle: The reasoning ability that enables us to acknowledge potential personal wrongness.

Impasse: What occurs when no mutually satisfying solution can be found. An impasse may be healthy or unhealthy.

Love: The actions involved in changing conflict systems, from bad to good.

Martyr: Unreasonable people's drama roles where they play the part of one who is rescued or victimized by others.

Master: Unreasonable people's drama roles where they play the part of one who must take control.

Maturity gap: The discrepancy between how mature we are and how mature we should be.

Messiah: Unreasonable people's drama roles where they play the part of one who needs to rescue others.

Mute: Unreasonable people's drama roles where they play the part of one who is untroubled.

Perception problem: When one person assumes or sees the actions of another in an untrue or distorted way. An actual difference of opinion may or may not exist.

Preference problem: When differences of opinion collide.

Pressure problem: External issues and forces that drain people's energy they need to solve conflicts.

Preplanned response: A choice or path decided upon before a situation arises that enables us to counteract our natural inclinations to react.

Process problem: Button pushing or reacting instead of active problem solving.

Reason muscle: Reasoning ability that enables us to do the right things with personal wrongness.

Reasonable people: People who have the ability and willingness to participate in problem solving.

Rehash: The natural tendency to revisit and refight a previously unresolved argument.

Reliability muscle: The reasoning ability that enables us to follow our intentions with actual behavioral changes.

Responsibility muscle: The reasoning ability that enables us to feel bothered by our awareness of personal wrongness.

Safety boundaries: Limits that keep us safe from dangerous (level 3) unreasonable people.

Unreasonable people: People who lack reasoning abilities, unable or unwilling to participate in conflict resolution. Unreasonable people deal with conflict by staging dramas.

Validation: What we receive or give that acknowledges opinions and feelings have been heard and understood. This may or may not mean agreeing with the other person.

Win–win: The conflict solution that satisfies the interests of both sides.

INTEGRITY
MANAGEMENT RESOURCES

Integrity Management Resources (IMR) is a management consulting firm specializing in:

strategy development,
security enhancement,
relational improvement,
and spiritual well-being.

Mike Henry President
Ray Goff Executive Vice President
Dr. Alan Godwin Senior Vice President

Visit our website at
www.trustimr.com